1978

PEOPLES OF THE EARTH

volume **1** Australia and Melanesia (including New Guinea)

volume **2** Africa from the Sahara to the Zambesi

volume **3** Europe (including USSR west of the Urals)

volume **4** Mexico and Central America

volume **5** Islands of the Atlantic (including the Caribbean)

volume **6** Amazonia, Orinoco and pampas

volume **7** Andes

volume **8** The Pacific – Polynesia and Micronesia

volume **9** Southern Africa and Madagascar

volume **10** Indonesia, Philippines and Malaysia

volume **11** South-East Asia

volume **12** The Indian subcontinent (including Ceylon)

volume **13** China (including Tibet), Japan and Korea

volume **14** USSR east of the Urals

volume **15** Western and central Asia

volume **16** The Arctic

volume **17** The Arab World

volume **18** North America

volume **19** Man the craftsman

volume **20** The Future of Mankind. General Index

volume eleven

South East Asia

THE DANBURY PRESS

(Preceding page) Most of the
people of South-east Asia
adhere to Buddhism.
Monasteries top the banks
of the slow-flowing Irrawaddy
as it meanders through Burma.

Editorial Director **Tom Stacey**

Picture Director **Alexander Low**
Executive Editor **Katherine Ivens**
Art Director **Tom Deas**
Assistant Editor **Elisabeth Meakin**
Project Co-ordinator **Anne Harrison**
Research **Cheryl Moyer**

Specialist Picture Research **Jeanne Griffiths**
Picture Research **Claire Baines**
Elly Beintema
Diana Eggitt
Carolyn Keay
Emma Stacey
Editorial Assistants **Richard Carlisle**
Rosamund Ellis
J. M. Marrin
Charlotte Nasim
Susan Rutherford
Pamela Tubby
Editorial Secretary **Caroline Silverman**
Design Assistants **Susan Forster**
Richard Kelly
Cartography **Ron Hayward**
Illustrations **Sandra Archibald, Ron McTrusty**

Production **Roger Multon**
Production Editor **Vanessa Charles**

The DANBURY PRESS
a division of GROLIER ENTERPRISES INC.
Publisher
ROBERT B. CLARKE

© 1973 Europa Verlag

The series has been created by Tom Stacey Ltd.

Library of Congress Catalog Card No. 72 85614

Printed in Italy by
Arnoldo Mondadori Editore, Verona

The publishers gratefully acknowledge help from
the following organizations:
Royal Anthropological Institute, London
Musée de l'Homme, Paris
International African Institute, London
British Museum, London
Royal Geographical Society, London
Scott Polar Research Institute, Cambridge
Royal Asiatic Society, London
Royal Central Asian Society, London
Pitt-Rivers Museum, Oxford
Horniman Museum, London
Institute of Latin American Studies, London

PHOTOGRAPHIC CREDITS
Cover – **Raghubir Singh** (The John Hillelson Agency), **Marc Riboud** (Magnum from the John Hillelson Agency), **Bruno Barbey** (Magnum from the John Hillelson Agency, **Syd Craiker** (F.P.G.). 2, 3 – **Raghubir Singh** (The John Hillelson Agency). 14, 15 – **R. Cagnoni** (Report). 16 – **Marc Riboud** (Magnum from the John Hillelson Agency). 17 – **Felix Greene** (The John Hillelson Agency), **Lee Lockwood** (Black Star, New York), **R. Cagnoni** (Report). 18, 19 – **Bruno Barbey** (Magnum from the John Hillelson Agency). 20, 21 – **Felix Greene** (The John Hillelson Agency). 22 – **Lee Lockwood** (Black Star, New York), **R. Cagnoni** (Report). **Marc Riboud** (Magnum from the John Hillelson Agency). 24 through 26 – **Howard Sochurek** (The John Hillelson Agency). 27 – **Syd Craiker** (F.P.G.). 28, 29 – **Howard Sochurek** (The John Hillelson Agency). 30, 31 – **Jean-Dominique Lajoux, Howard Sochurek** (The John Hillelson Agency). 32, 33 – **Howard Sochurek** (The John Hillelson Agency), **Syd Craiker** (F.P.G.). 34 – **J. H. Pickerell** (Colorific). 35 – **Howard Sochurek** (The John Hillelson Agency). 37 – **Jean-Dominique Lajoux**. 38, 39 – **Syd Craiker** (F.P.G.), **Howard Sochurek** (The John Hillelson Agency). 40, 41 – **Willy Mettler**. 42 – **William Hubbell** (F.P.G.). 43 – **Marc Riboud** (Magnum from the John Hillelson Agency), **Willy Mettler**. 44, 45 – **Marc Riboud** (Magnum from the John Hillelson Agency), **J. H. Pickerell** (Colorific). 46, 47 – **Anne de Henning** (The John Hillelson Agency). 49 – **Marc Riboud** (Magnum from the John Hillelson Agency), **Anne de Henning** (The John Hillelson Agency). 50 through 59 – **Philip Jones Griffiths**. 60, 61 – **James Pickerell** (Black Star, New York). 62, 63 – **Marc Riboud** (Magnum from the John Hillelson Agency), **James Pickerell** (Black Star, New York), **Don McCullin** (Camera Press). 64 – **Paul Stephanus** (Black Star, New York). 65 – **James Pickerell** (Black Star, New York), **Ian Berry** (Magnum from the John Hillelson Agency). 66 – **Jean-Dominique Lajoux**. 68 – **Marc Riboud** (Magnum from the John Hillelson Agency). 69 – **Don McCullin** (Camera Press). 70, 71 – **Ernst Haas** (Magnum from the John Hillelson Agency). 72, 73 – **Marc Riboud, Bruno Barbey** (both Magnum from the John Hillelson Agency). 74, 75 – **John Bulmer**. 76 – **Graham Keen** (Transworld), **P. Carrère** (Snark International). 77 – **John Bulmer**. 78, 79 – **Charles Moore** (Transworld), **William Macquitty**. 80, 81 – **Charles Moore** (Transworld), **Marc Riboud** (Magnum from the John Hillelson Agency). 82, 83 – **Marc Riboud** (Magnum from the John Hillelson Agency). 84 – **Boutin** (Snark International), **Keystone Press, Raghubir Singh** (The John Hillelson Agency). 85 – **Ivan Polunin**. 86 – **F. Walther** (Pictor Ltd.), **Pierre Ivanoff**. 87 – **Raghubir Singh** (The John Hillelson Agency), **P. Carrère** (Snark International). 88 – **Marc Riboud** (Magnum from the John Hillelson Agency). 89 – **Harrison Forman**. 90 – **William Macquitty, William Hubbell** (F.P.G.), **Harrison Forman**. 91 – **Marc Riboud** (Magnum from the John Hillelson Agency), **Raghubir Singh** (The John Hillelson Agency). 92 through 95 – **John Everingham**. 97 – **Thomas Höpker** (The John Hillelson Agency), **P. Carrère** (Snark International). 98, 99 – **Charles Moore** (Transworld). 100 through 103 – **Raghubir Singh** (The John Hillelson Agency), exc. bot. rt. 103 – **Charles Moore** (Transworld). 104, 105 – **Charles Moore** (Transworld), **Micha Bar-Am** (Magnum from the John Hillelson Agency), **Raghubir Singh** (The John Hillelson Agency). 106 – **Raghubir Singh** (The John Hillelson Agency). 107 – **Nicholas Fenn, Raghubir Singh** (The John Hillelson Agency), **Peter Smart**. 108, 109 – **Raghubir Singh** (The John Hillelson Agency), **Micha Bar-Am** (Magnum from the John Hillelson Agency). 110, 111 – **Raghubir Singh** (The John Hillelson Agency), **Bob McFarlane, John Bulmer**. 112 through 119 – **Pierre Ivanoff**. 121 – **Jørgen Bitsch**. 122 through 125 – **Peter Kunstadter**. 126 through 129 – **Peter Hinton**. 130, 131 – **Stewart Wavell**. 132, 133 – **Mavis Ronson** (Barnaby's Picture Library), **Stewart Wavell**. 135 – **Mavis Ronson** (Barnaby's Picture Library). 137 – **Stewart Wavell, Tom Stacey, Dennis Holman**.

Contents

Supervisory Editor of the Series:
Professor Sir Edward Evans-Pritchard,
Fellow of All Souls, Professor of Social Anthropology,
University of Oxford, 1946-1970,
Chevalier de la Légion d'Honneur

Volume Editor:
Andrew Turton, MA (Cantab),
Lecturer in Social Anthropology, School of
Oriental and African Studies, University of London

8–11   Unwritten literature
        Dr Ruth Finnegan, Faculty of Social Sciences,
        The Open University, author of *Oral Literature
        in Africa* etc

12–13   Peoples of South-east Asia
        Andrew Turton

14–23   People of North Vietnam
        Mo Teitelbaum, School of Oriental and African
        Studies, University of London

24–39   Proto-Indochinese (Montagnards) –
        Vietnam and the Khmer Republic
        Professor Georges Condominas, Directeur des
        Études, École Pratique des Hautes Études, author
        of *L'exotique est quotidien* etc

40–45   People of Laos
        J P Haarhoff

46–49   Yao – North Vietnam, Laos and
        Thailand
        Dr Jacques Lemoine, Chargé de Recherch, CNRS,
        author of *Un village Hmong vert du haut Laos*

50–59   People of South Vietnam
        Mo Teitelbaum

60–69   Saigonese – South Vietnam
        Mo Teitelbaum

70–77   People of Cambodia
        Lek-Hor Tan, School of Oriental and African
        Studies, University of London

78–81   Buddhism in South-east Asia
        Dr H Inagaki, Department of the Far East,
        School of Oriental and African Studies,
        University of London

82–91   People of Thailand
        Andrew Turton

92–97   Meo – Vietnam, Laos, Thailand
        and Burma
        Dr Jacques Lemoine

98–111 People of Burma
        C Skinner, School of Oriental and African
        Studies, University of London

112–119 Moken – Burma
        Christopher Derrick, author of *The Delicate
        Creation* etc

120–121 Padaung – Burma
        Christopher Derrick

122–125 Lua – Thailand
        S M Tylor

126–129 Karen – Thailand
        R Kennedy Skipton

130–135 Shan – Burma
        R Kennedy Skipton

136–137 Negrito – Thailand and Malaya
        Christopher Derrick

138–144 Glossary to the peoples of
        South-east Asia

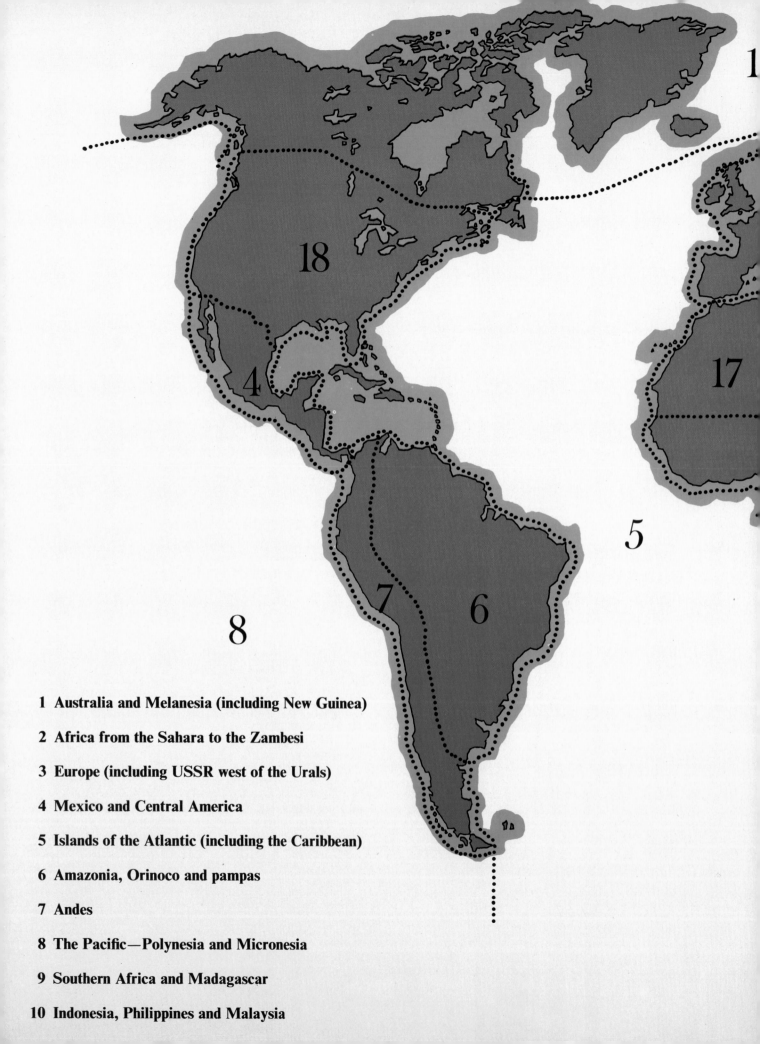

1 **Australia and Melanesia (including New Guinea)**

2 **Africa from the Sahara to the Zambesi**

3 **Europe (including USSR west of the Urals)**

4 **Mexico and Central America**

5 **Islands of the Atlantic (including the Caribbean)**

6 **Amazonia, Orinoco and pampas**

7 **Andes**

8 **The Pacific—Polynesia and Micronesia**

9 **Southern Africa and Madagascar**

10 **Indonesia, Philippines and Malaysia**

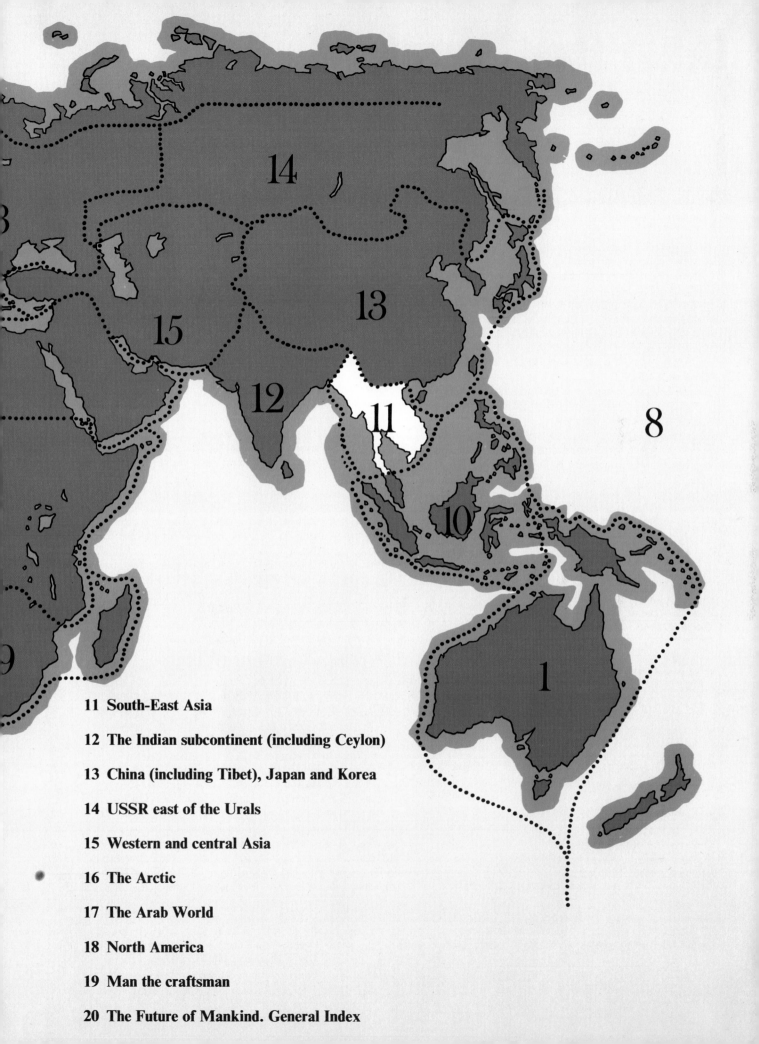

11 South-East Asia

12 The Indian subcontinent (including Ceylon)

13 China (including Tibet), Japan and Korea

14 USSR east of the Urals

15 Western and central Asia

16 The Arctic

17 The Arab World

18 North America

19 Man the craftsman

20 The Future of Mankind. General Index

Unwritten literature

It is not always recognized that the written word is only one form in which literature can be expressed and passed on. For centuries in the history of man literature has been composed and communicated without writing. And today there are many millions of people throughout the world—in the south sea islands, African tropical forest or savanna, the frozen ranges of the far north, the central Asian steppes, and many other places – who have little or no access to the riches of written literature, but who nevertheless possess a complex and subtle literature expressed in oral form. This unwritten literature, or 'oral literature' as it is usually called, includes many different forms: long heroic poems and epics for instance, love poems, panegyrics, elegies, lyrics of many kinds (the original meaning of 'lyric' was a poem to be sung), fables, stories, myths, lampoons and mythological chants.

No study of the peoples of the world can be complete without considering this widely distributed oral literature. When this literature is overlooked – as it too often has been in the past – one tends only to have a very external view of all these non-literate cultures and individuals. It begins to seem that men in these cultures that lack reading and writing must be unreflecting and childlike and lack any articulate or individualized thoughts or emotions and have at most only the most rudimentary traces of a literary art – formed largely by the dead hand of a long tradition or by a merely functional reaction to a social necessity. What is overlooked is that non-literate cultures do have a literature. They therefore do have a medium through which people can express emotion in accepted artistic forms. Through the medium of literary language they can meditate on the meaning, the humor and the sorrows of things.

Differences of culture and language can make it difficult for a foreigner to appreciate some of this oral literature. Fortunately there are many cases where an example of oral literature, although not performed for the special occasion for which it was intended, but rendered by a translation written down on a page, can convey something of its quality. Take, for instance, the Gond love lyrics from central India.

The mangoes grow in clusters,
O laden is the tamarind.
As near as seed to fruit,
So close should be our love.

But life is short, and death comes too soon:

What is man's body? It is a spark from the fire
It meets water and it is put out.
What is man's body? It is a bit of straw
It meets fire and is burnt.
What is man's body? It is a bubble of water
Broken by the wind.

As with literature anywhere themes of love and death tend constantly to recur. Even through the surface barriers of unusual imagery or foreign forms these lyrics can touch us – like the Somali *balwo* lyrics:

I long for you, as one
Whose dhow in summer winds
Is blown adrift and lost,
Longs for land, and finds –
Again the compass tells –
A gray and empty sea.

and

Your body is to Age and Death betrothed,
And some day all its richness they will share:
Before your firm flesh goes to feed their lusts,
Do not deny my right to love you now.

Again, this famous Zulu lyric laments old age briefly in words that have a wider appeal than just to the audiences to whom it was first sung:

The body perishes, the heart stays young.
The platter wears away with serving food.
No log retains its bark when old,
No lover peaceful while the rival weeps.

There are many other themes. Any object or event – local or universal, personal or social, anecdotal or philosophical – seems a potential topic for comment: the latest political move by central government or local bigwig, a football match, the mysterious origins of the world or of the gods, the love of children, the ways of women, struggles with the elements, the praises of the dead and of the living, the joys of the hunt, the esoteric pronouncements of oracles, the beauties of nature, the heroic deeds of warlike men of old, or just the ways of the world. The list is endless. The Zulu, for example, sing lyrics about love or declaim the glories of long poems about the past and songs about the present experience of living under an administration they find oppressive. Among the once-despised Ainu of Japan there is the epic *Kutune Shirka* about 'the golden sea otter', as well as the many women's narrative songs – usually about how some man is madly in love with them! The Winnebago American Indians relate their *waikan* myth cycle – a satire on man and Winnebago society, and a sacred tale about the primordial past. The Kazakh of Russian central Asia have as well as lyrical narratives about two young people's struggle for happiness together, a long tradition of lengthy epic poems about their national heroes and battles against their enemies. And the Yoruba of western Nigeria have their ponderous historical praise narratives, esoteric and deeply allusive oracular poems, hunting chants (marked by the occasional obscenity), as well as light-hearted satirical songs, humorous stories, and all kinds of political poetry.

In each oral literature many different literary genres can be recognized, each with its particular type of content, structure, style and, in some cases, musical framework or accompaniment. Among the Yoruba, for instance, at least eleven different genres of poetry have been distinguished. For the Somali there are even more different poetic genres and various dance and work songs as well.

The tone of oral literature is by no means always solemn, let alone necessarily religious in mood or context. An Eskimo poet, for instance, contributes a mocking epigram:

I have grown old,
I have lived much,
Many things I understand,
But for riddles I cannot solve.
Ha-ya-ya-ya.
The sun's origin,
The moon's nature,
The minds of women,
And why people have so many lice.
Ha-ya-ya-ya.

Many other Eskimo songs by contrast express a deep emotional feeling for nature around them. There are too the mystical cosmological themes of some Maori poetry. For the Maori, in one poem, the first of the six periods of creation was 'the epoch of thought':

From the conception the increase,
From the increase the swelling,
From the swelling the thought,
From the thought the remembrance,
From the remembrance the consciousness, the desire . . .

It is hard not to accept that formulations like these – although unwritten in their original form – indeed constitute 'literature', and a literature which can effectively communicate emotion and meaning right across the barriers of culture and language. There are many other examples – like the prose narratives or elaborate heroic epics which are so highly developed in many parts of the world – several eastern European and central Asian peoples, for example – that they are comparable with the early epic poetry of Homer.

This oral literature is communicated on many occasions. Sometimes a poem is not only composed but also recited by the poet when he is completely on his own, without an audience, particularly when long solitary periods are a necessary part of his life. So in the East African savanna Nuer and Dinka herdsmen chant poems of praise and glorification of their cattle as they pass long hours in lonely pastures:

. . . Friend, great ox of the spreading horns
Which ever bellow amid the herd,
Ox of the son of Bul
Maloa.

There are many other occasions when literature is sung or spoken. A mother sings a lullaby. Hunters celebrate their success. A group of children passes the time by exchanging verses or stories. A young man makes a satirical poem to comment on his employer behind his back. Or – a common occurrence among the Maori for example – a woman retaliates in a specially composed song to a criticism by her husband. Oral literature pieces are most commonly delivered within a group or to an audience. Songs sung within a group may be work songs which are often sung to accompany and lighten long monotonous work like hoeing, threshing, pulling trucks, marching, canoeing, grinding or launching a boat. The whole group usually sings to a chorus together, and a leader initiates each new verse, often improvising or embellishing it as he goes along. The evening is frequently a time when, after the day's work, people settle down to story-telling, often largely for the children's benefit. Sometimes even riddles and proverbs can be quoted or exchanged in a literary form. On these occasions the words may have many hidden functions. Riddles and proverbs may be intended to educate their audience or acquire prestige for an individual or a group of people. But their obvious immediate function is clearly simply recreational and aesthetic. This is also true of the widespread practice of holding poetic competitions. These may, as with the Tuareg or the Eskimo, be associated with warfare or settling disputes. But most often they are simply organized occasions for entertainment and display, as in several parts of East Africa, and among the Kazakh and Turkic-speaking Koibal of Siberia, and at the Polynesian singing contests which have helped foster poetry in the Pacific. Sung poetry is often part of the various ceremonies which mark the different stages of life. It is common to celebrate the stages of birth and death, initiation and marriage, and the festivals of the year, by performing poetry and music. At these times oral literature can enhance and make an occasion beautiful – and, quite simply, give people pleasure.

Oral literature is, too, often used for more specific purposes. Lampoons and satiric poetry are frequently employed by people to attack their opponents or to persuade someone to change his ways. The Chopi of Mozambique can put ambitious men in their place with public songs. This is 'poetic justice' used to democratic effect. And Ibo women have often persuaded an offender to reform his habits or pay up a fine by their virulent and often obscene lampoons. This sort of pressure is extremely common, and can take the form of direct political attacks on people in authority. These attacks can be highly effective – like this Somali poetic complaint about a sultan's dictatorial acts – which led eventually to his deposition:

The vicissitudes of the world, oh 'Olaad, are like the
clouds of the seasons
Autumn weather and spring weather come after each
other in turn . . .
. . . When fortune places a man even on the mere hem
of her robe,
he quickly becomes proud and overbearing
A small milking vessel, when filled to the brim, soon
overflows.

The diction and genre follow the conventional canons – but the overt purpose and occasion are political. Oral literature is also often associated with the pomp and 9 circumstance of religious or political authority.

There are occasions when panegyrics and set prayers are chanted or sung to the gods by specially trained priest-poets. These sacred narratives are often told and re-told on religious occasions. And with kings and chiefs the legendary stories which sanction their power are related on ceremonial occasions, especially during in-auguration rites. Court poets, charged with the duty of composing and delivering panegyrics of the leaders and transmitting the authorized historical and genealogical narratives are a common institution. Each Zulu king or chief, for instance, had his *imbongi* or praiser. The Ashanti and Hausa courts in West Africa had teams of praise poets and minstrels. And there were usually court poets in the kingdoms of medieval Ireland and Wales.

In some societies such lengthy and specialized heroic or epic poetry has developed that it demands special occasions for its delivery. Sometimes it has to be delivered in instalments rather than all at once. Even then long periods have to be set aside for reciting and hearing it. Thus we hear of the Russian Yakushkov spending a whole half-day reciting a heroic poem about Mikhailor Potvk. There are the narrative poems about Gold Khan or White Moon in south-eastern Siberia which each take five to six hours to sing. And there are Yugoslav oral epics which extend to thousands of lines. Performances on this scale are probably held in long evening sessions or on days kept free of normal work – for some listeners at least. Or they are held during special festivals which last several days like the thirty nights of Ramadan, or the classical Greek festivals which provided an opportunity for reciting the Homeric epics.

The narrators and poets of this oral literature vary among different societies. In some societies, just as there may be little specialization in any sphere of activity, there is little or no specialization in literature. Everyone is expected to be able to produce poetry, song and story, although certain individuals may be accepted as being more gifted than others. In other cultures people with some degree of expertise are recognized, perhaps in one particular literary and musical genre, rather than across the whole area of oral literature. People who are highly skilled are invited to attend and perform at particular ceremonies. These talented performers are not pro-fessionals. Their way of life tends to be basically the same as that of most of their fellows. Although oral literature has its full-time professionals they tend generally not to live by their art. The most they are likely to make from their virtuosity is some additional income in the form of gifts, or some extra prestige.

Some composer-performers, however, do live by their art. In some societies there are specialized poets and minstrels. Specialized story tellers tend to be more rare – though common enough in the East: a street corner story-teller in Taiwan, for example, will always be well rewarded by his wide-eyed audiences. The poets and minstrels have

a special position attached to some court or shrine. More frequently they travel the country rather like medieval European troubadours, living entirely by their talents. The Hausa praise-poets of northern Nigeria roam from village to village, picking on prominent local individuals to honor with their praises. If the expected reward is not forthcoming they damn them instead with poetic innuendo and invective. The 'griots' of Senegal, trouba-dours of Mauretania, and Muslim bards of eastern Europe do the same thing. These poets are often regarded ambivalently. They are feared for their power, and ad-mired for their art. They are despised for being in a sense only on the fringes of society, but given safe conduct and respect even in times of war.

Training and controlling specialist practitioners is not always left to chance. Poets sometimes form a special group which has its own methods of admission and training. There was the privileged grade of poets in early Ireland, for instance, and the Irish bardic schools. There were the highly organized, monopolist élite of Rwanda in central Africa. And there were the famous Maori 'schools of learning' which were closed to members of lower class families, and where only those who passed the initial tests were admitted to the higher grades of learning. Even if part-time experts who practise oral literature from time to time are more common there is, in non-literate societies, sometimes an intellectual and literary class who enjoy the prestige and position of their specialized talent.

These poets and narrators in non-literate societies are not, as is often supposed, necessarily subject to blind tradition. Their literary art is similarly neither always uncompromisingly functional nor directly determined by the needs of their society although literature and the people who communicate it vary in this respect from place to place. Claims of established authority and set rituals are more dominant over some poet performers, as in the case of many court poets, than over others. And oral poets and narrators, like any artists, naturally work within their own cultural tradition using its conventional genres and style. Naturally this does not rule out indi-vidual originality and inspiration. There are many recorded poems and stories in which it is clear how im-portant individual creativity has been. This is borne out by statements of some of the artists themselves. The gifted Eskimo poet Orpingalik, for instance, describes the elusive process of composing a new song: 'Man is moved just like this ice floe sailing here and there out in the current. His thoughts are driven by a flowing force when he feels joy, when he feels fear, when he feels sorrow. Thoughts can wash over him like a flood, making his breath come in gasps and his heart throb. Something, like an abatement in the weather, will keep him thawed up. And then it will happen that we, who always think we are small, will feel still smaller. And we will fear to use words. But it will happen that the words we need will come of themselves. When the words we want to use shoot up of themselves – we get a new song.'

The Kara Kirghiz oral epic singer explains his ability rather differently: 'God has implanted this gift of song in my heart. He gives me the word on my tongue, without my having to seek it. I have learnt none of my songs. All springs from my inner self.' The long and deliberate process of composition among the Gilbert Islanders of the south Pacific has been described by Grimble. There an inspired poet spends several days in the throes of composition. Although he may have some help from friends, it is mainly in solitary reflection that he composes his own song.

The creators of oral literature have, just like writers of literature, to work within local conventions of style and structure for their particular literary genres. Some literary genres demand long effusive high-flown language. Others demand highly compressed imagery and expression (the Somali 'miniature' lyrics for instance). Others still, like many West African animal tales, require everyday language interspersed with lyrics. Poets must use accepted poetic techniques, some of which may be highly complicated. They must use appropriate dialogue, soliloquy or chorus, metaphor, irony, rhetoric, parallelism – or whatever the appropriate literary convention happens to be. To this extent the poet or narrator is constrained in his originality. But it is these conventions that at the same time give him the opportunity to exploit them to create his own unique composition.

Scope for individual creativity comes out also in the performance of oral literature. If a literary piece is unwritten it is only through performance that it can be realized and communicated. The poet/reciter has a crucial part to play. In his performance he often acts as a composer as well as a mere voice for the words of others – although it is true that there are some occasions on which a reciter transmits more or less word for word what he has learnt from others. This tends to be particularly true in the case of religious language – like the Vedic literature which is said to have been handed down word for word over centuries. But generally it seems that the poet and speaker often composes in the very act of performance, especially in the case of narrative poetry. He puts together conventional themes, words, or phrases but combines and uses them in his own way, making up his own literary piece, a piece moreover which is unique to him on that one occasion. Among Yugoslav oral epic poets in the 1930s for instance, it was found that even the same poet would sometimes sing the 'same' song differently on different occasions. And when one poet learnt a poem from another, although he would say he was repeating it exactly as he heard it, he in fact introduced many differences not only in detailed wording, length and embellishment, but also in whole episodes. I have heard the 'same' plots of stories told by two different storytellers in northern Sierra Leone which showed striking

differences. There were differences in the names of the characters, the detailed order of episodes, the ending, the lyrical passages and, indeed, in the whole tone. Similar observations have been made for many other examples of oral literature, and the creative part played by the performer of oral literature is now generally recognized – not only in his way of performing, tone of voice, gesticulation or musical ability, but also through the stamp of his own personality on the actual words and ordering of his material. It is therefore now considered doubtful that most of our examples of oral literature have come down to us unchanged over many generations providing links with the supposed primeval tradition of past ages. Instead we must regard oral literature as a living art among the people who practise it, something to be understood largely in terms of their contemporary life.

Oral literature is not something strange and unusual, only to be found among backward or traditional peoples, inevitably bound to die out with the spread of modernization or of literacy. The existence of oral literacy forms in western urban society should make us rethink this assumption, which has undoubtedly been made. There are the modern protest songs, football and army songs, nursery rhymes, pop songs and the various offerings of radio and television – much of which could, in one sense at least, be classified as a type of oral literature. Indeed in the history of western civilization it is only fairly recently, with the advent of mass literacy, that transmission of literature through the printed word has become the norm. In classical antiquity and in medieval Europe oral delivery, even of written forms, was an important mode of publication and transmission. Similarly verse and stories originally drawn from written sources circulate in oral form among non-literate peoples in Africa, Asia and the Pacific, as the performer yet again makes his unique personal contribution and turns the piece into his 'own'. Again, existing oral forms are in many cases turned to new uses. Traditional military or narrative genres can be used for contemporary political struggles. Lyrics are used as a significant part of election campaigns among largely non-literate electorates, and even governments try to enlist oral poets for their own purposes. The Tanzanian government, for instance, sought the aid of minstrels to spread its new policies of socialism and self-reliance. The radio is a frequent vehicle for approved oral forms. And the Soviet authorities have used the traditional Kazakh poet to express and propagate the ideals of a new social order.

All in all, it seems unlikely that oral literature must die an automatic death even with the advent of full mass literacy – an event that is anyway still some time away for many people of the world. For many years still, people will continue, through the subtle vehicle of their oral literature, to delight in the beauty of words, philosophize, scandalize, amuse, pressurize, teach, beguile, and comment on the new and the old.

11

Peoples of South-east Asia

Three great rivers rise in the Tibetan plateau to the north of the Himalayas: the Brahmaputra, the Mekong and the Yangtze Kiang. The Brahmaputra flows south and west into the Indian Ocean, the Yangtze east and north into the China sea. The area between these two giant rivers is perhaps the widest definition of what we can call mainland South-east Asia. For many of the peoples or cultures now found further south originated close to the Yangtze basin. Through the center of this area, from north-west to south-east, flows the mighty Mekong linking China and Burma, Laos and Thailand, the Khmer Republic and Southern Vietnam. It does not link them very practically, for the rivers are seldom navigable over long stretches because of rapids.

In this part of the world it is the sea that unites; land divides. The hinterland is mountainous, thickly forested, malarial, and occupied by many independent peoples whose co-operation and friendliness could not in the past always be taken for granted.

It is along the coasts or not far inland in the delta regions that the ancient kingdoms of this part of Asia established their capitals and trading ports which linked them to the Buddhist religious centers of Ceylon and southern India, and to the imperial port of Canton. And it is here that we find the capital cities of today: Rangoon, Bangkok, Phnom Penh, Saigon, Hanoi.

Great cities have to be fed before they can trade and build fine palaces and temples. These same deltas provided the food – universally rice, grown in irrigated paddy fields. Here the farmers could rely on natural flooding in normal years thanks to the monsoon rains: gentle and manageable flooding in the Chao Phraya delta of Thailand and the Mekong delta of Southern Vietnam, but violent and destructive in the Red River delta of Northern Vietnam where thousands of miles of dykes and canals are needed, much of which were already built by 1800 AD. Such complex irrigation works need equally complex forms of social organization, requiring considerable co-operation between villages and a high degree of technological expertise.

The agricultural basis of these civilizations cannot be over-emphasized. The great majority of the people are still farmers; only some 10 per cent or so of the populations live in towns of any size. Indeed it is now thought that agriculture may have developed here thousands of years ago, independently of the 'fertile crescent' of Mesopotamia. And these farmers have a tradition of considerable independence from such few towns and cities as there were. They were also craftsmen, making their own looms and clothes, their pots and baskets, jewelry and iron tools, and building their own skilfully constructed and decorated houses and temples. These crafts were not so concentrated in the cities as in Europe. Fine cities certainly existed when English sailors first arrived in old Siam. Early in the 17th century they found the capital Ayuthaya as grand a city as their contemporary London. But the cities were above all the ritual and symbolic centers of these Asian kingdoms. When the power of the state declined the city might be abandoned – as in the case of the magnificent ruins of Angkor Wat in the Khmer Republic.

For some four thousand years there has been a continual movement of peoples of their cultures from north to south. The truly original peoples were assimilated, or exist only in tiny pockets of a few hundred people such as the Negrito peoples of the Peninsula. The first newcomers were the Malayo-Polynesia speakers who probably arrived by sea, and are now mostly found in maritime South-east Asia: Indonesia, Malaysia and the Philippines. These peoples gave way to the Mon-Khmer speakers. At its height the Khmer Empire (800-1300 AD) centered near Angkor Wat, held sway over most of the mainland area. Then, well within the Christian era, came the Tibeto-Burman speaking peoples to the west, and further east the Tai speaking peoples: Shan, Lao, Tai and Siamese (Thai). Members of all these language groups are to be found in both the mountainous regions and in the valleys.

In the valleys, as we have seen, they practised a settled form of agriculture and, influenced by Indian ideas of divine kingship and by Buddhism, they established kingdoms of great territorial extent with complex social hierarchies. In the hills and forests, which cover rather more than half the map area, wet rice cultivation is almost impossible. Instead we find the characteristic form of agriculture known as 'swiddening' or 'slash-and-burn'. Hunting and gathering forest products are also of considerable, though not primary, economic importance. These hill peoples are more mobile, and their forms of social organization tend to be less extensive than those of the valley. They do not form even small states. Nor do we find the influence of Buddhist or Hindu ideology in the hills. Yet we should not regard these minority peoples as isolated or without their cultural achievements. Traditionally there were quite complex trading relationships both within the hills and between hills and valleys. Hill people often played an important part in the ritual installation of valley kings and princes, and where valley power was weak such peoples as the Kachin, Karen and Lua established their own forms of aristocracy and chieftainship.

In parts of South-east Asia these so-called minority peoples together form a very large proportion of the population. In Burma, southern China, northern Laos, and northern and north-western Vietnam they enjoy considerable autonomy and are gradually, at their own pace, being drawn into the political, economic and cultural life of their countries.

There are many cultural similarities among nearly all the people of mainland South-east Asia. This is partly due to similar origins in the distant past and partly to their environment. Theirs is a world of rain and mud, or very varied and fast growing vegetation where stone and metal are at a premium and cattle are not herded in great numbers. So wood and grasses, creepers and fibers form the chief materials for toolmaking, building and clothing. Vegetables are the chief ingredients of the sauces and curries eaten with rice. For added protein there are the fish, and small birds and insects which abound in forests, streams and the flooded fields. This is the daily food – not the meat of domestic animals, which are kept for work, or as prestige items for ritual exchange between groups of men and for sacrifices for the world of spirits.

Beliefs and customs also show great similarity: beliefs in multiple souls, or life forces, for instance, that inhabit the human body and other forms of animal and plant life; belief in the magical power of tattooing; and beliefs concerning childbirth.

The term South-east Asia has only been in use since World War II, when it defined a strategic command zone. For centuries the region has been defined in this way by external interests. For the Chinese and Japanese it is the Nanyang or southern ocean; the British, French and Dutch came eastwards to 'Further India', 'French Indochina' and the 'Dutch East Indies', the Spanish and Americans extended their colonies westwards via the Philippines. The countries of South-east Asia have fought hard for their independence and today there still exist a wide variety of political forms: monarchies, military dictatorships, parliamentary republics and emerging socialist states. But the possibility exists of a regional community with its own identity and interests; a community of independent, sovereign, multi-national states, in which all the many peoples described in this volume might share, transforming their traditions and building new social forms.

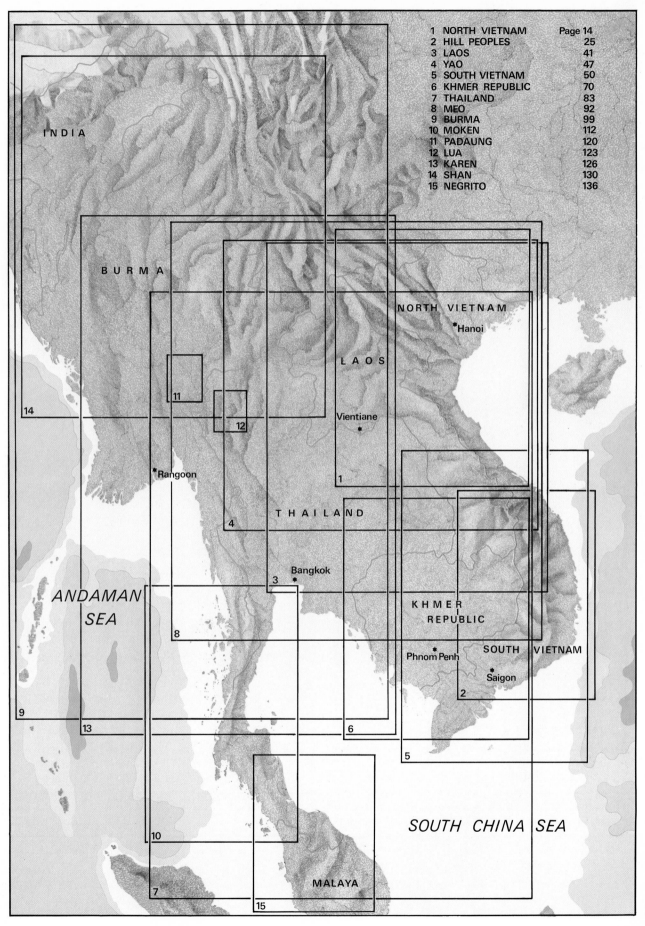

1	NORTH VIETNAM	Page 14
2	HILL PEOPLES	25
3	LAOS	41
4	YAO	47
5	SOUTH VIETNAM	50
6	KHMER REPUBLIC	70
7	THAILAND	83
8	MEO	92
9	BURMA	99
10	MOKEN	112
11	PADAUNG	120
12	LUA	123
13	KAREN	126
14	SHAN	130
15	NEGRITO	136

INDIA

BURMA

NORTH VIETNAM

*Hanoi

LAOS

Vientiane
*

*Rangoon

THAILAND

Bangkok
*

KHMER
REPUBLIC

Phnom Penh
*

SOUTH VIETNAM

Saigon
*

ANDAMAN
SEA

SOUTH CHINA SEA

MALAYA

14 · 11 · 12 · 4 · 3 · 8 · 9 · 13 · 6 · 5 · 2 · 1 · 10 · 7 · 15

People of North Vietnam

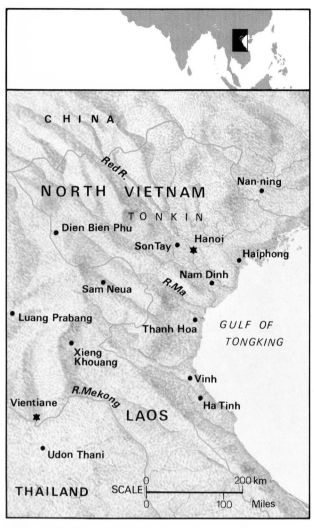

The division of the North Vietnamese and the South Vietnamese took place some five hundred years ago when the Viet people from the Red River area (today's North Vietnam) first settled the exceptionally rich delta of the Mekong, one of the world's greatest rivers, some thousand miles to the south. From that time the Viet people of the two wings began to develop their separate identities—despite inconclusive attempts by the northerners to establish authority over the southerners, at one time moving the northern capital to Hué, on the narrow neck of lowland linking the two parts of Viet territory.

The northerners are a hardy, ambitious and industrious people, challenged by a continental climate of cold winters and hot summers, and by the proximity of the traditionally mistrusted Chinese. The warmer, tropical, riverbound south has bred a more easygoing people with slower and gentler ways, speaking their own language with a markedly different brogue and with their own humor, folklore and style of life. For the northerners, the

15

Under Communist direction, dancing is extracted from its traditional setting to become — in this case — a lunch-time respite for Cam Pha miners.

The ruined town of That Diam has paid the penalty of a war with its origins in history. North Vietnam has always sought to dominate the south.

A Hanoi flower seller hauls a load of dahlias and reeds used in basket weaving. Bicycles are the most popular form of transport.

(Below) Under government supervision local dances are preserved as 'folklore'. Here they are put to use in a seamen's club in Haiphong.

Mekong valley has always been a coveted source of food.

In North Vietnam infertile, thinly populated mountainous stretches of land alternate with the fertile and productive lowland rural areas which are densely populated. In the plains which border the sea all down the coastline and in the lowland areas, live the people who represent 85 per cent of the population. These are the Viet (Vietnamese) or, as they are known to the neighboring minority peoples, the Kinh, or principal people. It was in the Red River delta, where they are concentrated today at a population density of 1,000 people per square mile, that the Vietnamese nation was first created and it was from here that the Vietnamese first began their expansion to the south. The Red River delta is known as the cradle of the nation.

The first recorded, authenticated details of Vietnamese history date from about 111 BC when the country was overwhelmed by the Chinese Empire. Yet the civilization of North Vietnam is often thought of as over 4,000 years old. Much of this early period is shrouded in semi-legend. Vietnam derives, it is said, from a kingdom known as Van Lang which was ruled by the Hong Bang dynasty for more than 2,600 years until 258 BC when the last Hong Bang king was overthrown. The second Vietnamese kingdom, also veiled in semi-legend and which only endured for 50 years was Au Lac. It was invaded and occupied by south-east Chinese armies in 207 BC – a date regarded by western historians as representing the beginning of the verifiable history of the Vietnamese. Au Lac was subjugated by the governor of a south-east China province inhabited mostly by Viet. The new state which was created, Nam Viet, extended as far south as a little beyond the Red River delta into northern-central Vietnam. In 111 BC, Nam Viet was conquered by the armies of the Han Empire. The land of the Viets became a Chinese province and remained so for more than 1,000 years.

During this period of Chinese domination, though not without opposition, it was in the Red River delta that the Chinese implanted much of their culture. They intro-

(Left) One-man concrete bomb shelters line a Hanoi street, reminders of the time when *may-bay-my*, US bombers, flew overhead.

(Over page) Years of toil in the Red River delta, protecting the rice crop from drought and flood, etch deep lines on a peasant's face.

duced the plow, draft animals, tools and other Chinese agricultural methods, as well as their customs and philosophy. They documented Vietnamese history. They introduced Confucianism in the 1st century AD (Buddhism came by way of Ceylon a little later between the 2nd and 6th centuries), and this became the central ideology of the Vietnamese nation. The Viet paid a high price for these benefits, but never allowed themselves to be assimilated by the Chinese, partly because of the long pre-Chinese history and the deep cultural roots of the Vietnamese, and partly because of the geography of their country.

It was against a background of disadvantages so gigantic that they seemed insuperable that the Viet settled in the Red River area. Indeed it is difficult to imagine how they did so. For the Vietnamese of the Red River delta are subject to some of the most devastating natural disasters. Flooding and drought plague their existence. In the Mekong Delta the South Vietnamese live in a far more pleasant climate. In North Vietnam there is a problem, which is the worse for plaguing what is today the most densely populated region of Vietnam. About 30 miles above Hanoi, the Black River and the Clear River disgorge their waters into the Red River which then carries 141,000 cubic feet of water per second through the 100 miles of the Delta from Viet Tri to the coast. In a year of low rainfall the volume of water may drop below 24,600 cubic feet and no water may reach the dry rice fields. In years of heavy rains, catastrophe falls upon fields and men. Excessive rainfall will cause the water of the Red River to rise up to forty times its usual volume.

Only through massive human efforts did the region of the Red River first become habitable and productive. It was necessary to tame the force of the river, channel the swollen waters into the river bed and store excess water for drought periods. This required a system of dykes, dams, and canals. The Red River now flows through the valley between two huge dykes. Some of these hydraulic works in the Red River delta are ancient. They were begun long before the independent state of Vietnam was established, and probably even before the advent of the conquering Han armies in 111 BC. Today the dykes cover an area of 1,600 miles and along them run some of the oldest roads of North Vietnam. These dykes were constructed by the labor of Vietnamese peasants. They certainly merit the description accorded them by the historian Buttinger as 'true ramparts of civilization'.

The Vietnamese are among the world's best rice growers. Wet rice agriculture imposes its own rhythm, a precise circle of economic activity, throughout the seasons of the year. In certain months a vast pool of labor is required for sowing and harvesting. At other times the peasants find themselves out of work. This pattern of intensive activity alternating with unemployment has tended to shape all social relationships. In order to survive people have had to co-operate not only as families – the basic working unit – and as villages, but

20

In villages without electricity, men use scoops to push water from an irrigation canal into a field of newly planted rice seedlings.

The fertile Red River delta, birthplace of the nation over 4,000 years ago, has shaped the Vietnamese into expert rice growers and skilled sailors.

Vietnamese lives are dominated by the rice crop. When the puddled fields are churned up before sowing everyone works from dawn to dusk.

(Below) Primitive but effective stone rollers thresh the new rice crop for the people of the densely peopled Red River delta.

relatively abundant natural fertilizers and beasts of burden, with a favorable climate. There is also a wealth of minerals: lead, zinc, iron, tin, bauxite and wolfram. The mountain rivers could be harnessed to provide a ready source of power.

All the nationalities and ethnic groups of Vietnam live in very different ways. Some have practised wet-rice agriculture for hundreds of years; some still carry on the primitive slash-and-burn agriculture and others live by hunting and fishing. Many are still at a semi-nomadic stage. At the time of the August Revolution of 1945, the various ethnic groups were at very different stages of development. While the Vietnamese, the Tay and the Nung had already reached an advanced stage of feudalism, the Tai, the Muong and the Meo were still dominated by their local chiefs. Each had its own original folklore, music, dances, decorative arts, oral literature and so on. Diverse religious beliefs were prevalent. The cult of ancestors was widespread in the mountains of the north and co-existed with animism, while fetishism was practised by many of the minority peoples of the Center. Many of these beliefs are still alive and flourish.

The Vietnamese of the plains and the mountain peoples have had dealings with each other for centuries. But there have been many attempts at divide and rule politics. In this country the Vietnamese monarchy used the Tay chiefs against the Nung. The French colonial régime used Vietnamese mandarins and police against the minorities. When Ho Chi Minh – whose army and political organization was superior to rival guerilla groups competing for power after the Japanese withdrawal in 1945 – assumed authority in Hanoi in 1954, he encouraged ethnic co-operation between the Vietnamese and all the minority peoples.

There are 37 officially recognized ethnic minorities in North Vietnam, a population of about 3 million beside the 17 million Vietnamese. Most of the minority peoples live in two great regions called Viet Bac and Tay Bac. Viet Bac was created as an 'autonomous zone' in 1956, and includes the five provinces of the north-east.

The largest of the minority peoples in all North Vietnam are the Tay who number about three per cent of the total population. Most of them live in Viet Bac. There is a theory that during the first millenium BC the ancestors of the Tay and the Tai, a branch of the Bach Viet who lived south of the Yangtse in China, emigrated south-eastwards to southern Yunnan and western Indochina. There is evidence that the Tai of Vietnam are closely related to the Tai who live in the south-west of China, in Laos, in Thailand and in Burma.

From the 4th century BC the Tai came to settle in small groups in North Vietnam. The Tai were one of these groups. In the 9th and 11th centuries AD they descended in much greater numbers, forming two great migratory currents, the first being the Tai and the second the Tay who are related to the Tai tribes of the Tay Bac

on a provincial and national level. The enormous amount of rice needed to feed the population of the Red River delta, for example, could not be produced without adequate irrigation and flood control. The dams, canals and dykes which had to be built were beyond the scope of the Vietnamese family and depended for their execution on national solidarity. This led to the very early formation of social structures which were to cement the Vietnamese people into a state.

Largely due to the fact that the Vietnamese live in deltas and along the coast – the vast majority live within 50 miles of the sea – they are skilled sailors and fishermen. They were once considered the best mariners of the Far East. Even those who live inland live close to a river. Wet rice, salt and fish are the staple, vital elements of the Vietnamese diet. But circling the fertile plains where the Vietnamese have for centuries cultivated wet rice there are 44,000 square miles of mountain country.

In these highlands live the minority groups of the North. They constitute about 15 per cent of the population. The lands where they live have always been considered strategically and politically important, but their economic potential has only just been discovered. There are vast stretches of forest, great water resources,

When most factories were
dispersed to the countryside
in small units this Hanoi
car repair plant kept
working through the war.

(Top) At 'Victory Co-operative
Farm', near Hanoi, girl clerks
study the cash books in the
evening. A fellow laborer
puffs a restful bamboo pipe.

Today's North Vietnam has
been built on an ethic of
war – as is vivid enough
from the toys on display
at a Hanoi state store.

A plantation worker taps the
bark of a rubber tree to
release the milky fluid latex
in the vast inland forests
west of the coastal plains.

region, but are generally thought to have migrated at a late date from southern China. The cultural difference that has evolved between the Tai and the Tay is mainly due to the fact that Tai retained an aloofness from the Vietnamese and correspondingly maintained their own traditional culture. The Tay, on the other hand, adopted a policy of communications and intercourse with the Vietnamese which is reflected in the inter-penetration of the two cultures.

The second largest minority group in Vietnam, the Muong, number over 400,000 and live mainly outside the two autonomous regions. They speak a language which is close to Vietnamese and which helped eradicate illiteracy among the Muong by 1960. The Muong have for some time adopted features of Vietnamese culture, and the only really distinct aspect of their own cultural life they have retained is their music.

The Tai are the third largest ethnic minority in North Vietnam. In 1960 they numbered less than 400,000 but by the end of 1965 their numbers had reached 446,000. They live largely in the Tay Bac region, although some live in other provinces. Different Tai groups living in different areas are known by a variety of names. They are called the Lu for example, near Dien Bien Phu, but they go by the name of Tay Deng, Tay Nuot and Tay Pong in the mountains of Nghe An and Thanh Hoa.

The Tai have long used advanced methods of farming, practising wet-rice agriculture like the Vietnamese. Unlike the Vietnamese, however, they only take in one harvest a year. The Tai are also familiar with the plow and with raising cattle, poultry and pigs. They are talented in handicrafts, especially weaving, and have not only their own rich folklore but their own script, with which they transmitted their culture from generation to generation. The Tai people have a passionate love of art and literature, of poetry, song and dance. Theirs is a deeply lyrical poetry which tells of young love and beautiful landscapes. And although they jealously guarded their separate identity and culture, the Tai have consistently joined with the Vietnamese and other ethnic groups in the fight against foreign domination. Their resistance was particularly strong in the first years of French colonization when for many years the Tai were in rebellion. In 1954 the government initiated a single writing system for all Tai groups, derived from Pali.

The Chinese population, with about 200,000 the seventh largest minority group, mostly live in the provinces of Quang Ninh, Ha Bac, Lang Son and Ha Giang. They have in the last 30 years moved closer to the Vietnamese culture. Most of them are fluent in Vietnamese and virtually all have now adopted Vietnamese citizenship since an agreement reached between the two Communist governments in Hanoi and Peking in the mid-1950s. They represent families which have been in Vietnam for a considerable time as descendants of Ming refugees. The Chinese government encourages the Chinese in North Vietnam to consider themselves as Vietnamese, which is why so few of them cling to their Chinese nationality.

Most of the ethnic minorities in Vietnam, except for the Tai, used to practise shifting cultivation. Today, in response to administrative and technological changes, over 70 per cent of them are organized into settled communities, many of which have been moved out of their traditional highlands to lower altitudes. Many still do live, as they always did, high up in the mountains. But a majority of the 200,000 strong Meo now occupy more lowlying territory in the north-west region of the Tay Bac. They are hardworking, tough and accustomed to hardship. There are five main Meo groups all of whom speak essentially the same language. A common language was worked out for all Meo groups in 1957, and has since been revised.

In 1967 the Yao, who are also called the Zao or the Man people, numbered some 200,000. They too have left the remote highlands and have had to grow accustomed to living at middle altitude. The Yao live over a greater part of North Vietnam than any other national minority. In spite of the differences and distance between the various Yao groups, the Yao form a community which is united by the same language and the same folklore. They are Chinese in origin and have a Chinese-derived language which the Hanoi administration encourages them to use. It would seem, from oral accounts and from traditional sources, that the Yao entered Vietnam in the 14th or 15th centuries. They are a proud people with a strong sense of independence which has led them into rebellion against both the Chinese mandarins and the French.

Ethnic harmony, called for in the first constitution of the Democratic Republic of Vietnam, is not easy to achieve. Above all there is the problem of creating economic improvements and social developments while still allowing some autonomy and continuity of culture. In general the Vietnamese of the north have shown greater respect for the dignity and equality of minority peoples than have their neighbors to the south, or in Laos or Thailand. They have shown greater understanding of their various histories and cultures, and of the need for different peoples to develop in their own time. There have been some heavy handed mistakes, which the Vietnamese have recognized and corrected. In the lowlands for instance there was the too rapid and centralized land reform program of 1955 with much unnecessary loss of life. This must be seen against the background of the colonial legacy of 1945 when two thirds of the peasants were landless and two million died of starvation in one year. By 1957 agricultural policy was changed and by 1968 over 94 percent of peasants had organized themselves into farming cooperatives; two and even three rice crops a year was the rule; and agricultural production had more than doubled.

23

Proto-Indochinese (Montagnards)
Vietnam and Khmer Republic

In a monsoon-flooded river
of highland Vietnam, a Mnong
boy holds fish in his mouth
and hand while groping for
more under water.

The remote villages of the hill tribes of South Vietnam have often been used as sanctuaries by guerrillas. In time of war these villages have provided recruiting centers for rebellion. It happened during World War II when the Japanese occupied South Vietnam, and it happened again in the long years of the Vietnam War. The villagers, who are called the Montagnards, frequently found themselves sheltering Viet Cong guerrillas, and at other times welcoming South Vietnamese troops. The hill tribes were caught in the wars of South-east Asia – wars which seemed to them to belong to other people. Refugees have told of Viet Cong making promises: 'Revolution will bring autonomy to all who support it' they said. But then the guerrillas began to take food and to draft the young men of the village. Other villages refused to become involved and built fences with bamboo spikes around their houses; some were even forced underground. The war has not respected the Montagnards' desire to be left alone, removed from the ways and life of the lowland Vietnamese.

25

Montagnards Vietnam and Khmer Republic

Low cloud hangs over the forest-covered mountain homeland of the Jeh, one of the thirty or so hill tribes of Vietnam.

A Mnong walks back to his hut – built on the ground unlike the huts of other hill tribes – carrying water from the river in clay pots.

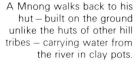

Journalists and English-speaking troops during the Vietnam war have used the French word *Montagnards* to describe the hill peoples who live in the Annamite hills on the South Vietnam-Cambodia border. The word describes the very people André G Haudricourt and I have baptised the Proto-Indochinese, a word analogous to the Proto-Malay and referring to Indochina in its original meaning of continental South-east Asia.

Until recently the peoples who live in the Annamite hills were called by several different names in different languages. So the Vietnamese, particularly guides who escorted anthropologists and field workers, called the hill people *Moi* which means savage. And Lao guides would call them *Kha* which means slave. In fact the only term which was not derogatory was the word *Phnong*, used by the Khmer and meaning simply hill people, or Montagnard. The people who live in the areas of the Cambodian-Vietnamese frontier which overlap the territory occupied by the Jai were referred to by all these three names. The small group living in Cambodian territory (Khmer Republic) came into contact with a minority group of people who spoke Thai and therefore gave them yet another Thai name. It is because of the marked differences between the ways of life and beliefs

26

All hill peoples consume enormous quantities of tobacco smoked out of elongated copper or bamboo pipes, and they chew betel.

(Opposite) With her child in front and a bundle of wood on her back a Jarai woman hurries home. Winters are cold: in the north it sometimes snows.

Montagnards Vietnam and Khmer Republic

Two fortified Jeh villages
perch on the tops of the green
hills of highland Vietnam from
which strangers can be
spotted more easily.

Like most Vietnamese the
Mnong's staple food is rice
but they like to eat pork
or water buffalo, here dressed
in a red spicy sauce.

of the hill people in relation to the plains people that the hill people were called by such, usually pejorative, names.

The distrust and denigration with which any group will refer to other, different, groups was intensified by two factors. On the one hand most of the hill people live in the forest, which the plains peoples fear. On the other they believe in and practise different religions. It is in the southern part of the Annamite range (between the 18th and 11th parallels), a relatively inaccessible area well protected by mountains that the Proto-Indochinese have most effectively succeeded in preserving their common cultural heritage.

Most of the Proto-Indochinese speak languages belonging to the Austro-asiatic (Mon-Khmer) group. But there is also a large group of various tribes, such as the Jarai, the Rhadè and the Churu, who speak dialects that derive from the Austronesian (Malayo-Polynesian) group of languages. These tribes live firmly ensconced in a remote corner deep in the center of the high country that overlaps into Cambodia north of the Cambodian-Vietnamese border. To the south of these Austronesian-speaking peoples there are different groups, the Mnong and Maa, and the rice-growing Lac and Sre. To the north there are the Bahnar, Sedang, Jeh and Katu.

Very few of these peoples are real nomads. The only two nomadic peoples among them comprise a few rare

All the hill peoples weave
beautiful cloth, either worn
as skirts or used by the
women to wrap their babies in.
The men wear simple loincloths.

29

The hill tribes consider
incisor teeth too doglike.
The top ones are knocked out
or filed down at puberty, the
lower ones filed into points.

Most hill peoples build their
houses on stilts and their
steeply sloping roofs enable
the rain to run off easily,
preventing damp.

groups which have been spotted in the chalky mountain
block north of the Ataouat, in an area which crosses the
Lao-Vietnamese frontier. These tiny groups live by
gathering, fishing and small game hunting, and build
simple shelters from leaves. The Lao call them Kha or
even Phi (meaning 'spirit') Tong Luang, which means
'of the yellow leaves'. The vast majority of these
Proto-Indochinese are shifting slash-and-burn farmers
whose whole way of life revolves around swiddening,
which provides them with their basic food, rice, or if
they are poor like some of the Mnong Cil, maize. Yearly,
or every two years, the farmers let the land they have
cultivated lie fallow, so that the soil can recover and be
enriched again by the forest. This means that entire
villages have to uproot themselves regularly, to cultivate
new or refreshed land. Villages uproot themselves even
more frequently for religious reasons.

In the marshes formed by the curve of the Daa' Doong
river one comes upon a group of Maa people who
practise a particularly archaic kind of paddy field
cultivation. They irrigate and cultivate the rice according
to an elaborate technique which they inherited from the
Cham, either preparing the ground with swing plows (as
with the Lac and the Sre) or simply employing buffalo to
trample it (as with the Mnong Rlam and the Bih). Except
when, as is rare, they are tight for space, irrigated rice

30

A little boy of the Bahna
tribe gazes out from
a hill ridge in his large hat
and short cloak of
dried leaves.

31

A girl of the Jarai tribe
pounds rice in a huge mortar
amid stylized figures carved
from wood probably for
sacrificial occasions.

A man of the Jeh tribe has laid out his knives for sharpening. He uses them for carving, felling and splitting trees and hunting.

A child sleeps contentedly on its mother's back while she molds clay pots which will bake in the sun and be used in the house.

cultivation does not supersede swiddening. For swiddening, or slash-and-burn, remains the supreme farming method; indeed in most cases it is the only method by which the mountainous land can really be worked at all.

Rearing stock also plays an important role in the daily lives of these people. All the animals which they raise, they rear not to eat but expressly for sacrifice. It is only when the animals are sacrificed that they are eaten. Everywhere they breed poultry, pigs and dogs – as guard-dogs and for hunting – and above all buffalo, not only for farm work, but as the supreme sacrificial beast. In some places they also rear goats and saddle-horses – the only animals which they never sacrifice.

Capturing and training elephants have given the Mnong of Ban Don a very special reputation. For them elephants are an important source of income, as the possession of elephants is to all hill people the infallible sign of a special prestige.

As well as farming to produce their staple foods and rearing animals for sacrifice and incidental consumption, by gathering, fishing and, to a lesser extent, by hunting these people appreciably supplement their diet. And apart from plants which they cultivate for raw materials

to produce goods like cotton and indigo it is in the forest that they can find all they require for building materials and basketwork materials. Tree bark beaten out to produce barkcloth has throughout the region survived the introduction of cotton but is not all the same generally used now except when there is a lack of cloth. It is now principally used for making elephant mattresses.

Women of most tribes use cloth to make their mid-calf-length skirts. Men usually wear loin cloths which they wind between their thighs and leave a section hanging down in front before finally winding it a few times around their loins. Women, like men, usually go naked above the waist, but for feasts and when it is cold they put on short or medium-length tunics with or without sleeves. They also have beautiful blankets in which they carry their children on their backs.

For jewelry, of which they wear a great variety, there are notably the ivory bottle stoppers worn by the Mnong and the Jarai and the spiralling boar's tusks worn by the Katu and obtained by the same technique as the same decorations are obtained in the New Hebrides. In the majority of tribes where they have preserved their traditional dress people still mutilate and lacquer their

Firewood is stored
beneath a hill home of wood,
thatch and plaited reed walls.
It is a small home compared to
the huge Rhadè long houses.

A brother and sister take a
rest on their wooden bed.
Corn cobs hang from the
roof and sunlight filters
through the plaited walls.

All through the hills people sacrifice bulls on festive occasions. This ceremony was in honor of visiting Viet politicos from Saigon.

(Center) Men excite the bull by dancing round with drums and cymbals before cutting its tendons through above the hocks.

The bull, at last unable to stand, is run through with spears. The more the animal suffers the less likely are the evil spirits to cause harm.

This ceremony takes place
at the village of Phi Di Ya
after the rice harvest. A water
buffalo awaits its fate under
an altar fringed with bamboo.

At the climax of the feast
the bull, hocks sticking
through its skin, is singed
on bamboo stems before it is
divided among the villagers.

teeth. They file away the top front teeth completely, but file the lower front teeth down to a point – a custom which was without doubt formerly an initiation rite but which today has only aesthetic significance. People also sporadically tattoo themselves. The most remarkable tattoo motif is used by the Katu: a stylized representation of a woman performing a ritual dance.

A number of men wear turbans, but in many tribes they, like the women, wear their hair coiled into chignons. It is in their chignons that the Mnong Gar and the Maa stick their iron pocket knives, with curved iron handles, which they are never without. The most important of all Montagnard tools, however, is a knife with a long handle curved close to the blade, with which they cut down trees and which they carry over their shoulders. They prefer a weighted axe for chopping down big tree trunks.

In all these activities the hill people have overcome technical difficulties or inadequacies by helping each-other. The different jobs in the fields are done by groups. Houses are built in the same way. People set off together in groups to gather food and to bring in the buffalo. And fishing and hunting are much more productive if done collectively rather than by individual enterprise.

The hill peoples have a closed economy. Each household produces all the clothes and utensils it needs. There is, however, some regional specialization. The Sedang and the Kuoy of Cambodia, for example, extract iron ore from the minerals with which their country is richly endowed. The Mnong Gar provide their rice-growing neighbors, the Mnong Rlam and the Lac, with the clothes which their wives do not know how to weave, exchanging them for buffalo which they are unable to rear on a large scale.

Even within a tribe there are villages which alone have potters who can model the pots and bowls that everyone needs. As for possessions which show an individual's wealth and power – the Montagnard equivalent of status symbols – objects like urns, gongs, bronze pots and other less precious commodities like salt and cheap wares are sold to them by Cambodian, Laotian and Vietnamese peddlers. Either the peddlers come up to trade with the hill people, or the hill people go down to bargain with them in the plains. These goods, once obtained, become the object of much bartering among the hill people. The majority of the more coveted 'status symbols' have been circulating within the tribes from time immemorial. The most important of them have acquired a kind of 'pedigree' reinforced by a legend associated with them. Apart from elephants, which are used only by very rich people, the most usual method of transporting goods and objects is on the human back, in a basket.

Hill people's houses vary greatly, but are usually perched on stilts. A great exception are the houses of the majority of Mnong tribes who build enormous dwellings straight onto the beaten ground. A Mnong dwelling may only be small and shelter only the couple and their 35 children (as among the Mnong Rlam) or it may be immense and shelter all the wives of the clan represented in the village together with their husbands and all of their children – as among the Rhadè. With the Mnong Gar several couples linked by ties of family or simply of friendship may live together in one building.

Although water is what a Montagnard usually drinks he consumes a greater part of his paddy in the form of rice beer. If he wishes to honor a guest he will uncork a jar of this, offer it to him, and the guest will drink it straight out of the jar through a straw. The precious rice beer is also an indispensable drink at sacrifices. Like all Indochinese the hill peoples also smoke enormous quantities of tobacco. Their very distinctive pipes of copper but above all of bamboo are thin and often elongated. In some tribes the women chew betel, but have a particular predilection for chewing the frayed ends of the fine blades of bamboo which are used to clean out the pipes.

The institution of communal houses is generally widespread north, but non-existent south, of Pleiku. The communal house usually stands at the center of the village either with houses radiating all around it, as with the Brao in Cambodia, or else in two parallel lines on either side of a roadway leading to it, as with the Kaseng of south Laos. Or there may, as with the Lamet in north Cambodia, be no precise order at all. As for those tribes that do not build communal houses some build their houses in a specific pattern, others haphazardly.

Montagnard family units too are organized in the most different ways. But there was one type of family unit in particular which struck the first explorers in this region so forcibly that for a long time it was regarded as far more usual than it in fact is.

This is a harmonious clan system which distinguishes the Jarai, Rhadè, Churn and indeed all the Austronesian tribes including even the Cham, the coastal Indianized cousins of these people. It is a system shared not only by the Mon-Khmer speaking groups whom they have strongly influenced and by the rice-growing Sre, Lac or Mnong Rlam, but also the Mnong Gar. The people who live according to this system invariably marry outside their own clan. On marriage a man goes to live with or near his wife's family. And people trace descent through the maternal line.

But in general the Austroasiatic peoples both to the north and to the south of the Malayo-Polynesian group trace their descent both through their fathers and their mothers, occasionally, as with the Maa, emphasizing descent through the male line. There is even among the Mnong Prong a harmonious system by which descent is invariably traced through the father and married couples go to live with the husband's parents. There is finally, among the Pang Tieng, a system where descent is traced unilineally, through the mother's or father's line.

Although in many groups space for any social activity is confined to village territory, there is usually an easy balance between families. In other groups – particularly among the Austronesians – the clan will seize advantage of a distinctly privileged situation. Among all the hill peoples dominating tribes have on occasion sprung up, established authority over several villages and held on to it for varying periods of time before the villages revert, as they almost always do, to their customary independence. In north Laos, however, as much with the Khmu as with the Laotians themselves, the memory of a once-fabulously rich Kha kingdom survives. But the most original institution of this kind still remains that of the Potao – the famous *sadets,* or kings, of Fire, Water and Wind who held ritualistic exchanges with neighboring kingdoms, notably with Cambodia.

The religious institutions of these tribes rest on their belief in a multiplicity of souls and in the countless *Yaang* – all the spirits which people heaven and earth. Some of these spirits, the most highly developed of them, have come to exercise an important role which distinguishes them from the mass. Carrying out the rituals rarely involves anybody other than the members of the family. Even in the agricultural rites and in the rites involved in rebuilding a village carried out under the auspices of holy men on behalf of the entire village (which can go on without stopping for several days) the head of each household participates in his own right, in the presence and under the direction of the holy men.

The shaman, who enters into relations with the *Yaang* (spirits) and evil-doing sorcerers, called *caak,* is an important figure. Through the shaman's interpretation the sorcerers can demand any sacrifice they desire from a sick person. The shaman usually receives his initiation from another shaman, following an agreement contracted with the spirits, which is an agreement analagous to those that men contract with each other. Among the Sre and Raglai tribes and their neighbors the shamans are initiated at Boumong in Raglai country, and consecrated by a veritable pontiff of shamans who lives there.

The most important rites, those which are repeated regularly each year and upon which the survival and wealth of the household depend, are the agricultural rites which mark each phase of life in the fields. The animal of the noblest sacrifices, the most high-ranking victim of all, the property against which all property is gauged, is the buffalo.

The hill people usually bury their dead. No sooner has a man given his last sigh than he is presented with gifts and offerings of food – until his burial if he is Mnong for example, or, if he is Rhadè until the feast celebrating the final abandonment of the body in the tomb, which may take years after his actual death. With the Bih the skeleton is removed from the coffin before the final burial. Until then it has been lying on a pyre of pruned bamboo shoots. It is washed and the skull is carried around the village wrapped in a blanket, rather like a small child,

The Jeh tribe, like the other
hill people, carry their water
in long hollow bamboo poles.
Villages are built on high
ground: valleys harbor malaria.

37

Young Jeh children sit
amid the skulls and horns
of oxen which hang inside the
huts to ward off the
evil spirits.

Jarai women return from gathering firewood. Carrying loads is women's work. A thorn fence protects their long houses from wild beasts.

The traditional method of drinking rice wine is through straws straight from earthenware pots, but bottles in the background suggest innovation.

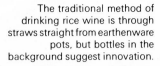

by an old woman.

All the tribes possess an oral literature which ranges from simple songs through folksongs and sequences of poems in which the traditions and wisdom of the group are distilled, to magnificent epic declamations. They have musical instruments of various kinds: all sorts of zithers, mouth organs mounted on gourds, horns made out of buffalo horn, big, double-skinned drums and above all, gongs – flat ones and convex ones – which because they represent wealth are nearly always grouped together as an orchestra.

Dances are often, as with the Mnong Gar, no more than a circular line of *cing* dancers moving one after the other around sacrificial posts and stakes or they may, as with the Samre, be elaborate ballets in which the dancers dress up as animals. The hill people are noted in the plastic arts for the beauty and fineness of their basketwork and fabrics. For sacrifices, particularly those which crown the funeral rites, they sculpt animals and stylized figures of men in wood, and cover ritual planks and stakes with geometric and figurative designs. Perhaps the finest expression of this art graces the tombs of the Jarai.

(Opposite) Water from the mountain streams runs down to Jarai villages in bamboo guttering and is collected in a communal trough.

39

A Christian cross is taken as a talisman to the house of an ageing villager. Christianity was recently introduced but people still believe in spirits.

People of Laos

40 The Kingdom of Laos is a
country of many festivals
and celebrations. Here
young girls, wearing precious
Lao cloths, take part in a fête.

The kingdom of Laos is a country almost exactly the size of Great Britain, though with a population of less than three million. About half the inhabitants are Lao or Laotian, a Tai people, and the other half consists of many minority peoples, also found in neighboring Thailand and Vietnam – Meo, Yao, Khmu, and others. Laos extends over 600 miles from north to south, bordered by mountains to the north and east, and to the west by the great Mekong river, which gives the country geographic unity. Its political unity, at times tenuous, dates from the 14th century AD when the Kingdom of a Million Elephants achieved some independence from the Khmer Empire. But the present political frontiers of Laos are the creation of the French, who established their colonial protectorate in 1885, and stayed until their defeat in 1954 at the battle of Dien Bien Phu just over the border in northern Vietnam.

Laos is watered by the wide Mekong river and its tributaries. The river contributes to Laos' rich fertility, and nourishes the sticky-rice and maize fields, the gently sloping table lands, and the forests at the water's edge. So rivers have come to have a great significance in Lao culture. The rising and falling waters both bring fertility 41

People of Laos

and carry away evil. The Laotians consign a scapegoat to the waters every year, which floats away guilt and troubles on the current. And they follow a custom which is widespread in Asian countries with monsoon climates. At the end of the eleventh month, the end of the rainy season and the end of the Buddhist 'Lent' or monastic retreat, people make little wooden rafts, put candles or lights in them and send them away down the river. The custom comes from a pre-Buddhist period and, like many Laotian celebrations and festivals, symbolizes a new spiritual start at the beginning of a new season.

Laotians are great fishermen and boatmen and often travel long distances by water — sometimes in long, graceful punts, sometimes in more modern craft. Fishing is a great sport: the Laotians use nets when they can afford them, or more often fishing spears, or simply their own teeth. There is even a fishing festival, near Vientiane at Ban Ang, when special fish are caught in special ways according to ancient beliefs which require the spirits of the water to be consulted and placated through a medium. Besides these festivals, the Laotians catch all kinds of fish for family consumption, eating them cooked, raw or preserved. Some fish are used as ingredients for sorcery and traditional curative medicines, which are just as popular as western therapy and more readily available. Some women for example wear the spine of a skate in their knotted hair to protect them

against the Phi Pop, an evil spirit.

The Laotians are primarily sticky-rice growers, although they are herdsmen as well, especially on the table lands. Villages are united in a system of mutual help – around crops of rice, tobacco, sugar cane and maize – and individual families also grow their own vegetables whenever possible. Beneath coconut trees bending their gray green trunks to the rivers, houses on stilts are built out of wood and foliage. When the rains come in June the villages are quiet because men, women and children are working in the rice fields. Later there will be more noise, especially the noise of weaving-looms coming from almost every house. Laotian weaving is not only an old and beautiful craft. It has started to become an important cottage industry and bright and intricate Laotian textiles are appearing on the world market.

Children play unrestricted, almost neglected, in the shade. Monks in their saffron robes endlessly pass through, collecting alms, or their dues, giving advice, discussing the affairs of the local temple. There is often a serenity that comes perhaps from Buddhist beliefs.

Buddhism was introduced to Sri Lanka (Ceylon) in the 3rd century BC and took on a particularly Sinhalese character. And it was from Sri Lanka that Theravada Buddhism (see pages 78-81) came back through continental India, Burma and Cambodia to the country of the Mekong. In Laos, as in all Theravada Buddhist

countries, the monks are respected and supported by the community. The monks teach that life is suffering, that a man's present existence is only one among many, and that a better rebirth, or ultimately the blissful extinction of desire, Nirvana itself, can only be achieved by doing good, both in an ethical sense, good behavior, or in a ritual sense, making sacrifices; as they say in Laos to do a *boun,* or make merit.

To honor and respect any temple and any image of the Buddha is to do a *boun.* To take offerings of flowers or rice cakes is to do a *boun.* To give freely to the saffron robed monks is to do a *boun.* Praying and self-prostration in the temples are merit-making and so is reflecting on one's own spiritual life. For every Laotian the year is full of religious observances, although these often become mixed with secular celebration, as at funerals or a New Year. After the spectacular New Year processions comes the festival for the departed, the candle procession of the eighth month, and the three lenten months of fasting, in which everyone goes regularly to the temples to offer lotus blossoms, to listen to sermons and to observe the Eight Precepts. Then in the ninth and tenth month of the Laotian calendar are Hokhaopadap Dinh and Hokhao Slak, further festivals for the departed – each as joyous as a western Christmas, or more so. Then comes the harvest festival called Pha Vet, when villagers celebrate the former lives of the Buddha, remembering his abandonment of all earthly things.

Even daily life has its religious order: gongs sound in the early morning to remind families to give food and alms to the monks. When this is done a Laotian can drink to the goddess earth, and eat. Children are entrusted to the monks to learn and to serve when they are about ten. In this way each Laotian has a *khru* or guru. Then monks also play an important part in naming new babies and they are almost always involved in the many thread-tying ceremonies which tie a bride and bridegroom together, or bind the corpse of a dead man. Religion, which is scarcely beginning to lose its sway, is still of

At the fête of Pi Mai in April
the king's royal elephants
are led in procession
round the town by finely
dressed royal servants.

Dressed in white the prince
passes on his birthday through
groups of kneeling courtiers
at his palace in ancient
and beautiful Luang Prabang.

43

People of Laos

In the New Year festivities Laotians build mounds of sand with signs of the zodiac on top, and wish for blessings as numerous as the grains of sand.

inestimable significance in the daily lives of the people of Laos, and religious practices account for a large proportion of a village household's annual expenditure.

Laotian astrologers divide their year differently from westerners. Theirs is a lunar year; the New Year falls in the fifth month, which is our April, and coincides with the rebirth of nature, when the country begins to turn green under April's first showers. On New Year's day everyone goes to the *wat* (temple) to sprinkle the Buddha with water and ask for prosperity and good fortune. Ordinary people, especially young people, wear their brightest clothes and sprinkle each other in the streets. Small mounds of sand are put up in the temples and on the banks of the Mekong, with paper streamers and signs of the zodiac on them, and their builders ask for blessings as numerous as the grains of sand. The royal prince of Laos frees birds from a cage as an act of merit. There is a special procession, in the royal capital of Luang Prabang, of the royal elephants. There is dancing and singing, which are both highly developed arts. From Luang Prabang the king makes formal visits to various temples, passing through lines of his subjects who sprinkle him with scented water. The king and other notables also give a *baci,* a ritual common to all Tai peoples, but especially highly developed in Laos.

44   A *baci* is a celebration of various things, and is also

Frogs, ants' eggs and cows' placenta are great delicacies. Frogs are often skinned alive, the skin is fried and the frogs are eaten live later.

A Lao boy proudly wears a T-shirt celebrating the US moon landing: behind him are some achievements of his own country.

called *sukhuan,* which means calling and welcoming the soul. People hold a *baci* at a wedding, after the birth of a baby, or at any particularly happy time which may also be a time of problematic transition from one social state to another. A lucky day and hour are chosen and the household prepares trays covered with banana leaves and flowers. These sweet-smelling baskets are laid out and the celebrant – preferably a former monk – comes and sits facing the guest of honor. Someone lights candles and incense and the celebrant summons the guardian gods. All kinds of food are offered to tempt the gods to send back lost souls – including any of the souls of the guests that may have strayed from their bodies. The Laotians believe that each of the 32 parts of the body has a soul. Then someone fastens a cotton thread to the celebrant's wrist, which he then attaches to the person in whose honor the *sukhuan* is being given. The audience, with their hands on their foreheads, murmur 'sa!', breaking the silence. Then the *sukhuan* develops into a night watch, or a court of love as it is called, where girls and young men whisper sweet nothings under the supervision of their mothers and the stimulus of plentiful drink.

Marriages are surrounded by customs which must be observed. Agreement is reached only after oblique and formal negotiations between the parents – a kind of elliptical giving and avoiding of compliments. On the day of the formal proposal the bridegroom's family sends young girls with the usual presents of betel nuts, tobacco, ricecakes and other offerings, to the bride's house. She is dressed in her wedding dress and she too goes through a ceremony of poetic and rhetorical questions. Then later the young man arrives for the thread-tying ceremony. Next day there is a *sukhuan,* and the little trays are often covered in gold and silver gifts.

Death and funerals are, rather oddly from a western point of view, occasions for happiness and celebration too. For a Buddhist death means the release of the spirit from the sufferings of earth, perhaps into a better existence. Soon after his death a person's body is washed with scented water, and a coin is put between his teeth to show how little of his wordly goods he needs or can take with him into death. Cotton threads twisted round his neck, feet, and wrists show how tenuous are the bonds holding man to the earth. For seven days the corpse is tended. While the monks pray the dead person's relations watch over the coffin. The young people dance and play riotous games in the shadow of death. Orchestras play and drink flows, and even close relations show few signs of grief, because that might hold back the dead man's soul. Then the coffin, especially if it is of a wealthy or respected person, is put in a special mausoleum, and kept till the fourth month, which is an auspicious time for funerals. The building, or *mem,* may have lively decorations and drawings – many of them fairly lewd – to show respect and happiness. Finally the body is cremated.

Birth is surrounded with ritual too. When a wife knows she is pregnant, she takes part in a ceremony wishing for many children. She has to observe many taboos; for instance, she must not eat larva from bees otherwise her baby might be as turbulent as bees; if she steps over the head rope of an ox or horse the child might be greedy; or if she dries her skirt in the sun the wrong way up, her child might be born upside down. The delivery is attended by a male midwife, or sometimes by a *mo sado,* or exorcist, and there are many invocations and magic precautions taken to protect the child from evil.

Thus Buddhist and other older beliefs are found side by side in the pattern of festivals, celebrations and rituals that mark the Laotian yearly calendar. The year is also marked by the all important monsoons and the rise and fall of the great river, which determine the agricultural cycle. For despite the disruptions of decades of fighting for independence, the influences of first French and now American culture in the towns, and the beginnings of small industries in the north, the life of the Laotian farmer continues in ways which have changed little for many centuries.

45

Yao
North Vietnam, Laos & Thailand

The Yao believe they are
the descendants of
P'an Hou, a dog who saved
the life of a Chinese emperor
and married his daughter.

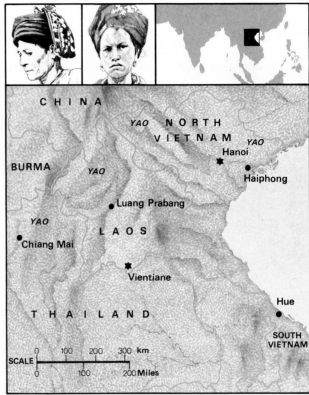

For many of the Yao peoples of South-east Asia, home in recent years has been where war has driven them. In the space of a man's life time he may have farmed in the mountains of Laos, and then in Thailand before settling in North Vietnam. Despite isolation and some security in the mountains, the Yao have throughout their long history been ill-starred in the fortunes of war. And yet the Yao have never abandoned the ways of their ancestors, nor have they forgotten their ancient traditions. To renounce these traditions would be, for the Yao, to hasten the end of the epic tale of the 'Blessed Descendants of the Twelve Yao Clans'. Opium is their livelihood: they grow the poppy and sell the drug it produces. Only adults smoke it, in moderation, but it sometimes becomes an indulgence among the old.

The Yao have links with an ancient period of Chinese history. According to the chronicles of the later Han Dynasty (20–220 AD), the emperor Kao Hsin (2435–2345 BC) had promised to give his daughter in marriage to anyone who could rid him of his enemy, General Wou, chief of the marauding Chuan Jong tribe. A five-colored dog, named P'an Hou, which he had housed in the court, succeeded in tricking and killing General Wou and brought back his head to the emperor. With a certain reluctance the Chinese emperor fulfilled his promise, and so the dog married the princess and took her away to 47 distant mountains. The children they had were to become the forefathers of the Yao tribe.

From such mythical beginnings the Yao became widely scattered in many parts of south China and developed a variety of local dialects, the most important being the Mien, the Mun, the Pu Nu and the Lakkja. The Mien group, the most numerous, was driven away from the Nanking area in the second half of the 14th century. In 1386 or 1387 a long drought forced the Mien to leave the coastal mountains of Chekiang, where they had retreated, and to embark in rented boats on the China Sea in search of better land, and they arrived finally in the mountainous district of Shaochow. This region became the starting point for their subsequent migrations to Hounan in the north, and Kweichow and Yunnan in the west. The voyage across the sea at the mercy of the waves became a second myth of origin for the Mien.

Mien society is divided into twelve clans, each composed of descendants of the six sons and six daughters of King P'an. The clans were further broken up into segments, partly as a result of the Chinese influence which forbade marriage within the clan.

The Mien like to keep the extended family together in the same household and to maintain lineage bonds whenever such households break up. The need for additional labor and a recurring problem of female sterility has induced them to adopt as many children as possible from neighboring tribes. The adopted children are treated as full members of the Mien society.

It is still not clear when the Mien were converted to Taoist religion and philosophy. Their Chinese religious teachers left them the Chinese writing system together with the main canons for Taoist ceremonies. They were able to incorporate their own legends into these rituals and soon developed a lasting passion for the Chinese verse form of seven feet. The art of writing is handed down from father to son, each generation copying out old texts to leave for their descendants. Their Taoism is strikingly integrated into their everyday life and completely independent of any modern Chinese influence, even though a Chinese calligrapher may sometimes be hired to teach the children and copy old books. When a boy reaches the age of 16 or 17 he is given a religious name to be used on such occasions as the ceremonial introductions to each level of the religious hierarchy.

After the second grade of this hierarchy, a man becomes a priest able to conduct the major ceremonies such as funerals and the different activities undertaken to 'pacify the ancestors' or deliver them from the prisons of hell. The priest has become an earthly representative of the Taoist pantheon, dominated by the Triad of the Three Pure Ones. The assembly of spirits is represented on paintings piously conserved in a basketwork box above the household altar. The master who has instructed the new priest then hands over a seal engraved with his rank, which he will affix to all the letters and documents he sends to the powers of the Beyond.

But even without reaching this level of initiation, many men learn the techniques of divination, and are skilled in the practice of exorcism and the recall of the soul. The search for wandering souls bears striking resemblance to Meo shamanism (see pages 92-97). Finally, at each level attained in the Taoist order, the new initiate acquires a small troop of Soldiers of the Beyond, handed over by the master to his disciple. These soldiers are themselves wandering souls who no longer have any descendants to offer them the appropriate cults and sacrifices, and who are recruited by the Taoist masters as their retainers in the other world.

The Mien are among the most careful slash-and-burn agriculturalists. By cultivating their fields in long rotation, they usually allow the tropical forest time to regenerate. They produce mainly rice for their own consumption and maize with which to feed their poultry and pigs. Opium provides most of their cash. It was first introduced after the Opium wars, fought against the Chinese by the British in the mid 19th century to establish a monopoly in the opium trade. Being able to save the money earned by the sale of their opium harvest, pigs and surplus rice, they may occasionally move down to the town and become merchants. The majority, however, prefer the isolation and security of the mountains. Having been forced to move frequently as a result of the Indochinese wars, most Mien have known two or three different countries during their life-time. They nevertheless live as faithful citizens, respecting the laws and generally appreciated by governments. Theft and murder are unknown, and all differences are resolved within the authority of the village.

Marriage is the great event in their lives, for marriage means children, by whom they fulfil their duties towards the ancestors. Young people meet freely, and sexual freedom is customary, but marriages are left to the initiative of the parents. The girl's family will be contacted through a go-between and if the destinies of the couple are compatible (according to the hour, day and year of their birth), the families exchange gifts and begin discussions. They must agree on compensation for the trouble taken by the girl's family in bringing her up, and for the loss of her assistance with production, and then they undertake the formalities of an engagement. When the boy's family has assembled the required number of silver bars, the marriage may take place. Some time may elapse between the engagement and the actual marriage, and a couple's child will frequently be present at the wedding ceremony. Since the young wife comes from another clan, or at least a different lineage, she must be presented to the ancestors and sometimes even 'pacify' them. A priest, who receives her at the main entrance of the house, undertakes to exorcise the evil influence which she might bring into her new home. When the spirits and ancestors have been appeased, it is time to prepare a great feast with music and wedding songs.

48

The Yao practise slash-and-
burn agriculture in their
mountain villages, where
the old ways are preserved
and crime is unknown.

Opium is the Yao's main
source of cash income. They
grow it locally and prepare
it in their huts for sale
to Tai middlemen.

Yao women dress beautifully
in embroidered clothes. Their
headdresses are particularly
rich with red and black
thread and silver chains.

Female sterility cause Yao
families to adopt many children
from neighboring groups.
They are treated as full
members of Yao society.

49

People of South Vietnam

Vietnam has been likened to two bags of rice dangling from each end of a pole. The vast majority – 90 per cent – of Vietnamese live in the two rice-growing regions of the Red River delta in the north, where Haiphong is, and the Mekong delta in the south, where Saigon is. In between these great wide deltas are nearly 1,000 miles of narrow coastlands, averaging less than 20 miles across, where wet rice growers live in small strung-out settlements. Inland the wild mountain regions are inhabited by hill tribes who have little to do with the lowland Vietnamese or Viet. The southern Mekong delta is more populous than the northern Red River delta but has been part of the Vietnamese nation for the shortest time.

Villagers cling to the very
edges of their land, over-
flowing into sampans on the
thousand waterways to make
room for precious rice fields.

The harvest is threshed by hand beside the flooded paddy field. Usually buffalo are used to thresh the rice underfoot.

Only in the 17th century was the area populated by the Viet. French colonial rule was established in 1859 in Saigon and soon spread to Tonkin (North Vietnam), Laos and Cambodia (Khmer Republic), comprising all of so-called Indochina. France's authority and presence were interrupted by the Japanese occupation of 1943-45, and were never securely re-established in the face of several armies of local insurgents. The end came at the battle of Dien Bien Phu in 1954, when the country was partitioned under communist rule in the North and on makeshift democratic lines in the South.

In spite of overwhelming changes during the last troubled century Vietnamese society holds fast to certain principles. Its kinship system, undying loyalty to the family, the Confucianist ethics of filial piety, the importance of the household rather than the individual, the practice of working together and helping each other still play an important part in those villages which have not been ravaged. The Vietnamese village was traditionally thought to be the anchor of the society, the foundation of the nation. As a self-contained unit it has throughout the centuries managed to retain a high degree of autonomy. The oft-quoted saying that the authority of the emperor ends at the gates of the villages is quite accurate. The village is an identity symbol, a protective association.

In South Vietnam most traditional village structures began to break down under the impact of the French colonialist drive for the export of rice. Before that the villages satisfied their own needs and stored surplus grain for a bad year. Households remained on their village lands for hundreds of years, rarely venturing beyond their confines. But this pattern has been brutally transformed by war and the massive removal of village populations into camps, Strategic Hamlets, orphanages for parentless refugee children, or for children of mixed American and Vietnamese unions.

Vietnam has been in existence as an independent kingdom for centuries under the domination of the powerful Viet. Vietnam became an independent state in the 10th century after 1,000 years of Chinese rule when the Viet defeat of the Chinese in 939 AD at last freed their country from foreign domination. They soon expanded advancing southwards beyond the confines of the vastly overcrowded Red River delta to the rice lands that lay beyond. The Viet freedom lasted, apart from a short 20-year period from 1407 to 1427 when the Chinese again held sway, until the French conquest of Vietnam in 1883. In 1407 about 90 per cent of present-day South Vietnam was not yet part of the Vietnamese state for the Viet had not then reached so far south.

The southward advance of the Viet lasted over 800 years. Bands of peasants farmed and fought, clearing land and already-established inhabitants in a bid for survival. The peasant soldier is an age-old institution in Vietnam. These Vietnamese bands of expansionists

(Left) Half a millennium ago bands of Viet peasants thrust south from the Red River until they reached their Eldorado, the fertile Mekong delta.

(Center) Coracles require skilful handling at any time, but to steer two at once you must be born the son of a fisherman.

She has seen war upset the peaceful rice-dominated life of her village; she may not live long enough to see the old rhythms return.

53

forged their way down the length of the coast as they searched out the rice lands, intruding into and acquiring the territories of the Cham, a semi-nomadic, Malayo-Polynesian speaking Indonesian people who were also fine sailors and knew how to exploit the sea's resources.

The Cham today number only between 20,000 and 40,000 in South Vietnam. Once they dominated the South-east Asian peninsula and lived all along the coasts of South Vietnam. Theirs is the heritage of the Champa Kingdom which came into being at the end of the 2nd century AD originating just below present-day Hué and soon expanding south and west for 200 miles into the Mekong Valley of present-day Cambodia and southern Laos. Today they are scattered in two pockets of the central region – the Phan Rang and the Phan Ri area in the provinces of Ninh Thuan and Binh Thuan – and some also live along the border with Cambodia near Chau Doc and Tay Ninh. The Cham are the only remaining vestiges of the once proud kingdom of Champa, the last sons of a proud and highly civilized nation which was defeated and expelled during the hundreds of years of wars between the Cambodians and the Vietnamese. Now their villages are poor and miserable.

The Khmer are another indigenous group that the expanding Viet would have encountered on their south-ward march. They once formed part of the great Khmer empire and therefore still have close linguistic and cultural ties with the Cambodians. They are descendants of those Cambodians who remained in the Mekong delta even after the expansion of the Vietnamese had resulted in all the southern provinces of Cambodia being annexed to Vietnam and now they are considered one of the major minority peoples of South Vietnam. Their communities are found in Tay-ninh, Tra Vinh, in the Transbassac and until recently the Camau peninsula – the very southern-most tip of the South-east Asian mainland. This peninsula suffered heavily from defoliation by the American army. Here the names of many towns recall Khmer origins: Soc-Trang, for example, which comes from Srok Khleang and means 'land of the granaries' and Camau which comes from Tuk Khmau and means 'black waters'.

The Khmer are Theravada Buddhists whose lives are based on fishing and wet-rice agriculture, and live mainly along the sands in huts roofed with palm leaves. Their huts stand on stilts and are surrounded by banana trees and coconut palms. Their communities tend to be less cohesive than Viet communities. They tend to group around the pagoda which is the focal point of village life – a center of instruction and leadership. They have a passion for poetry, music and the arts. Their women weave fabrics in bright colors and the men are skilled at jewel cutting and making decorated arms.

By pushing south in this way, the Viet through the centuries discovered fertile valleys down the long Viet-namese coastline to sustain their wet-rice agriculture. They eventually reached their Eldorado, the great rich

The fishing nets are left to dry in the sun while the whole family devote themselves to gathering in the rice harvest.

The monsoon breaks upon the Mekong, flooding the rice fields and heralding the beginning of a new cycle of plowing and planting.

plain of the Mekong River delta, which was larger and deeper than the Red River delta which they had left 800 miles behind them in the north. The migrating groups were made up of individuals and families, some who had left the north on their own incentive and others who had been sent by the state to search out new lands. The result was that lots of separate little communities developed, while an essential unity remained. The Vietnamese of the warmer Mekong delta in the south began to take on characteristics of speech and attitude that distinguish them from their brothers in the somewhat more temperate Red River delta in the north. The northerners, however, retained their presumption of authority among all Viet people.

The peoples the Viet encountered on their southward drive were either overcome, swept aside, like the groups of Khmer and Cham or assimilated by the superior Viet, who had the advantage of a long association with the Chinese from whom they had learned advanced knowledge and techniques. They were also a united people in contrast to those whom they found in their way. They spoke the same language and their unity was reinforced by deeply rooted beliefs and ancient customs. Moreover they were continually supervised and protected by their powerful state functionaries who were careful to ensure that the Viet should neither be absorbed nor influenced by the alien peoples with whom they came into contact.

It took from 1400 to 1780 for the March to the South to accomplish the vital and extensive leg of its advance from the Peak of Clouds south of Hué to the tip of the Camau peninsula. The occupation of the Mekong delta – up to 120 miles wide – was a gradual, continuous process for it absorbed far more people than the Red River delta had ever managed to support. And so the acquisition of this fertile delta was vitally important to the growth of the Vietnamese nation.

Although divided today the North and the South Vietnamese are alike. In both areas regions habitable by wet-rice cultivators are limited by mountains. The same pattern of a central delta – the Red River delta in North Vietnam and the Mekong delta in South Vietnam – and narrow fertile plains on the coasts dominates, and the same social structures exist.

Although many villages have been destroyed in the war, some remain as they have done for centuries and many have been rebuilt. In each village are a Buddhist pagoda and its shrine to the spirit considered to be the guardian of the community. Religious beliefs are linked to and stem from the rhythm of the rice-growing process.

Rites and rituals are attached to each stage of their work. Most families have an ancestral shrine in their homes. This too is often connected with the agricultural reality for an ancestor might become a deity for having left a legacy of fields or cattle.

Rice-growing is dependent on the seasons. From June to October the monsoon rains flood the fields heralding 55

The slab of wood inside this farmer's house is both table and bed — and, in war, a barrier against mortars and bomb splinters.

(Over page) The balmy tropical climate of the south makes life easy — but vulnerable to the ambitions of the colder north.

People of South Vietnam

Outboard motors have replaced
poles among the sampan
community on a tributary of
the Mekong at Sadec near
the Cambodian border.

the period of intense activity. There, village farmers with
their buffalos work in the mud plowing up the soil. At
this time the entire family works desperately hard, planting the rice seedlings. And so for about four months of
the year the village is hectically busy. Then comes a pause
while the rice grows and a time of unemployment sets in.
As well as the wet-rice agriculture which controls their
lives, villagers cultivate vegetable plots. They keep
chickens, ducks, pigs and cattle for their own family
needs. In most villages one will see buffalo and plow
working the fields separated by dykes. Increasingly one
sees the work done by tractors, left by the Americans.
Often in the past, and sometimes still, the buffalos and
other animals are owned jointly by the villagers.

At harvest time there is great activity. The old-
fashioned method is to cut the rice stalks with a sickle.
They are then transported to the central gathering point
in ox-carts where they are threshed by buffalo and oxen.
Villagers often spend calm evenings watching the buffalo
threshing the rice underfoot. Natural harmony is
important to the Vietnamese peasant and continuity is an
important element of this harmony. That is why ancestors
are often buried in the fields where their spirits may enter
the rice which is then eaten by the new generation.

Life for the villagers is simple and tough. They eat
two meals a day, one in the morning and the other in the
afternoon. Rice is of course the staple element. Those

who can afford it will supplement rice from time to time
with fish or meat. Although fresh fish is quite easily
obtainable the villager more often eats it dried and
unsalted. Most of the poorer peasants eat only rice with
the national sauce *nuoc mam* which is perhaps the most
famous of Vietnamese food. It is made of the strongly-
flavored and strong smelling juice of fermented fish.
Pork is the favorite meat of the villager and his diet is
supplemented by vegetables such as cabbage or beans.

The villages of the Mekong delta are set like islands
amid the paddy fields. Their houses are made of wood
from palm trees. Living accommodation is limited so
that all possible land can be used for cultivation. Many
houses are constructed on the edge of rivers and village
children learn to swim from birth.

One of the most tragic consequences of the war has
been the destruction of the traditional village-orientated
Vietnam. Hundreds of village headmen were systemati-
cally murdered by Viet Cong insurgents and North
Vietnamese invaders. Thousands of the country villagers
fled into Saigon as their villages and crops were destroyed.
Many of them went back again to try and carry on among
the ruins until the next wave of military activity, when
again they would seek safety in the already overcrowded
towns.

As well as the Viet, the Khmer and the Cham there
are 33 hill tribes who live in South Vietnam. They

inhabit the high-altitude areas, the highlands of central and South Vietnam, which extend from the border with North Vietnam down to Bien Hoa just north of Saigon, and the great flat Mekong delta area. Their skin color ranges from the lightest brown to darkest black. The highland tribes are said to bear a closer resemblance to the Indonesians and Filipinos than to the Vietnamese. Each of these tribes, which are racially very different and racially and linguistically distinct from the lowland Vietnamese, has its own language, customs, territorial areas and kinship systems. Conditioned by and totally dependent on their tough natural environment they have become over the centuries an entirely village based and orientated community. Unlike the Viets they remain unsubjected to a wider system of rule.

To the South Vietnamese the one million or so highland peoples are known as the *nguoi thuong* or the *nguoi Viet-nam Moi,* the 'highland citizens' or the 'New Vietnamese citizens'. They are in fact the oldest inhabitants of this part of Asia and as such are known as Proto-Indochinese by various experts, including Georges Condominas (see pages 24-39). The French referred to them as the Montagnards, or highland people, which aptly reflects their geographical identity. They are also known by the derogatory Vietnamese label *moi* which means savage, and by other pejorative Laotian and Cambodian terms *Kha* and *pnong*.

Their mountainous territory covered with dense jungle and rain forests is not suitable to the lowland Vietnamese dependence on rice cultivation. But the mountain area is huge. It covers more than two thirds of the area of South Vietnam and only a small proportion of the total South Vietnamese population lives there.

The Vietnamese, the ethnic majority of South Vietnam, have for centuries come into contact with various civilizations. They have assimilated and adapted various cultural influences and have pondered foreign concepts and ideas. The hill peoples on the other hand have remained in a state of isolation, neglected and often scorned. Little has changed in their traditional pattern of thought and behavior and the age-old superstitions have survived virtually intact. The marked differences between the lowland Vietnamese and the hill peoples are based on the geographic distance and language differences, but unlike the North Vietnam régime, the South has done little to overcome these handicaps.

The hill peoples have borrowed little from the Vietnamese of South Vietnam and the cultural differences between the tribes themselves are sustained by poor communications. Although the road networks around the cities are better than in most South-east Asian countries, the roads into the highlands are virtually non-existent. There is almost no cultural exchange, no intercommunal discourse. As a result of generations of almost unbroken isolation the two sections of Vietnamese society distrust and fear each other.

59

(Center) The village is quiet while the rice grows, but with the arrival of the harvest everyone becomes hectically busy.

The threshed rice is raked and winnowed to separate the grain from the light husk which is left to blow away in the wind.

Saigonese
South Vietnam

When the US forces left
Saigon, many of the 80,000
bargirls learnt touch-typing
or returned to their villages
with their savings.

During the last ten years the population of Saigon has multiplied ten times, making it the most densely populated city in the world. It has a population density two and a half times greater than Tokyo. These are statistics which point to human misery and the destruction of a culture based on social solidarity. The loss of its traditional cultural identity is instantly visible in its downtown foreign restaurants, bright lights, huge advertisements, juke-boxes, traffic jams and innumerable foreign-made vehicles. It is a consumer society, operating at fever pitch on an artificial injection of dollar resources. The massive publicity hoardings of the Saigon waterfront testify to the new, modern disease that spread its bacteria during the long war. Whether it is the growth of office blocks run up 'on spec' or the sad spectacle of cheap villas hastily erected to make a quick profit from transit Americans, the city tells of a false boom.

The word 'un-Vietnamese' springs to mind in relation to so many aspects of life in Saigon today. Beggars – a new and un-Vietnamese phenomenon – have proliferated. In the past Confucian and Buddhist ethics excluded large-scale persistent begging. The rich cared for the poor, the young for the old. The situation was never perfect, but it was never like the streets of Saigon today, which teem with mendicants, many of whom are war-veterans hobbling on crutches.

The beautiful Vietnamese dress of the traditional women, the *ao-dai* – simple, flowing, elegant and discreet – has been widely replaced by the more garish western fashions. The age of the mini-skirt, the pin-up girl, the nude pictures arrived in Saigon with the influx of foreign troops and has not left with their departure. Drugs have also become prevalent in the city. The Vietnamese have traditionally had a taste for the opium pipe, but never for the injected heroin which has been introduced into an alienated population, creating a tragic wave of juvenile addiction.

From a society which strained to respect the Confucianist principles of righteous living and integrity, Saigon has degenerated into a city of pimps, prostitutes, thieves and pickpockets. Pick-pocketing has become (although less lucrative now since the withdrawal of US troops) the obsessive pastime and the only means of survival of a considerable section of the errant population. Tiny pert little boys, and pretty, innocent little girls can actually be seen at it at various times of the day and night. The United States bases suffered most from petty thieving by their Vietnamese personnel – a situation which led to the most rigorous searches. It is a social phenomenon totally divorced from traditional Vietnamese ethics and the product of an imbalanced situation, a too-rigid contrast between flashily rich and miserably poor.

And if Saigon has become the mecca of pickpockets, it is equally the rubbish-dump of Vietnam. The Vietnamese are not accustomed to waste and pollution, for

Soon these opium smokers
will become somnolent and
remote, wafted to a
world far away from
their war-ravaged country.

in traditional society all manner of waste products were used for practical purposes. But that was before the consumer economy. Now the vast stretches of accumulated rubbish – the beer and Coca-Cola cans and cardboard boxes are the wretched hunting grounds of the deprived population. And in Saigon's central market stall-holders repaint old American army desks and sell them to offices. They also sell army boot lockers. The metal in these is in theory believed to be suitable for the body of Vietnam's only home-produced motor car, the Dalat.

Saigon also stands today as the symbol of the demolition of Vietnamese traditional agricultural society, for here, in the refugee camps, and among the rootless in the suburbs of the city, are the thousands upon thousands of displaced peasants. They signify the destruction of the strong bond which used to exist between villager and village. In anonymous herds the homeless people are relocated into camps where traditional family and kinship ties no longer operate. The close-knit peasant society has been bombed into urban solitariness.

The flower-market still lights Saigon with its brilliant colors but the contrast is even more striking as the cycle

Saigon's street markets have suffered in the competition with black market trading which the restrictions of war invariably bring.

Like cardboard boxes and Coca-Cola cans, Saigon's bars and dancehalls remain as part of the detritus of an alien 'go-get-it' society.

The American way of life
startled and excited the
young people of Saigon used
to the discipline of Buddhism
and oriental Catholicism.

Saigonese South Vietnam

rickshaws (cyclos), motor-scooters, Mercedes, Volks-wagens and Chevrolets shoot past. The old native stalls of Le Loi Street and Nguyen Hue Street now have to vie with the black-market vendors. Tastes had to be catered for and those tastes were not Vietnamese. Thus the cultural identity was transformed by commercial necessity and will perhaps never again be recaptured. For when a city has reached the pitch of consumer-orientation and congestion and degradation that Saigon has, the historical, traditional values are gone forever.

Vietnam has been described as the 'crossroads of civilization', a name which is particularly suited to Saigon, for it is a place of passage of many people, one of the bridges which links Asia to the west and to America. And for the South Vietnamese it is a point of contact between technological civilization and agricultural civilization. Throughout its history Saigon has witnessed many diverse events and has been visited and influenced by many different peoples. The Fou-nan, the Khmer and the Chinese have all at one time or another established themselves within the confines of the city. The French who colonized Vietnam brought African and Arab troops. And in World War II the Japanese came as invaders. Then it was the turn of America whose troops arrived in 1965 and who brought in their wake soldiers of many races. Australians, South Koreans, Thais, Filipinos – all have crowded the streets of Saigon.

Centuries of contact with Chinese culture influenced the theater where highly stylized plays are performed to the crashing of cymbals.

The dramatic rise in the population of Saigon-Cholon in the last twenty years has been caused mainly by political events. The Geneva agreement in 1954, which ended Vietnam's eight-year war of independence against the French, partitioned the country along the 17th parallel. Immediately there was a wave of refugees from the communist North which swelled the population of Saigon to one and a half million people. Then came the Vietnam war, and most observers now contend that the population of the city has reached over three million including all the refugees who have flocked there in the last decade, fleeing from the harassment and bombardment of the war. In 1969, as well as the Vietnamese, there were 500,000 Chinese concentrated in Cholon part of Saigon, 5,336 Saigon citizens of Montagnard origin, 6,575 citizens of Cham origin, and 46,210 foreigners of whom 10,328 were French, 9,607 American, 1,741 Indian, 689 Japanese and 509 English. Cambodians and Laotians are regarded as assimilated with the Vietnamese.

The people of Saigon are divided into various religious groups. The majority regard themselves as Buddhists, although they are not necessarily devout practitioners. Most others are devotees of Catholicism, Caodaism or the Hoa-hoa religion but a few remain under the influence of Confucianism and Taoism. The Cham community alone practise Islam, although the thousands of Vietnamized Cham who live in Saigon do not seem particularly devout in their observance. And hundreds and thousands of Vietnamese are non-believers, although the word 'atheist' does not have the same significance as it does in Europe.

The Chinese in Saigon hold a position of great strength and importance. The first Chinese to settle in Saigon in the 18th century were soldiers and officials who, deeply loyal to the Ming dynasty, had chosen exile rather than serve the new Manchu régime in China. In 1778 they established the Chinese district of Cholon in Saigon, which remains predominantly Chinese today. But it was during the period of French colonial rule that large numbers of Chinese workers were brought in as labor from south China, with the result that in 1937 the Chinese outnumbered the Vietnamese in Saigon. Today there are less Chinese than Vietnamese but they hold, as they always have done, all the key positions in commerce, industry, banking and in the artisan trades. More than 60 per cent of the businesses are in Chinese hands, and the Chinese play the most important role in the economic life of South Vietnam. The Vietnamese leaders are only too well aware of this, and would like to change it, but they remain impotent in the face of Chinese industry. Under President Diem the government did try to curb the economic power of the Chinese. They imposed heavy taxes on them and applied restrictive rules on their import and export business, but their measures failed because of the solidarity and cohesion of the Chinese community. The Chinese safeguard their interests and their prime

65

Incense is burned, fire-
crackers are lit and prayers
are offered to Buddha for a
successful New Year during
the *Tet* festival.

In Saigon religion and
politics blend and the
Buddhist, Caodaoist and
Catholic clergy wield
a great deal of power.

position in the Vietnamese economy with great efficiency, corrupting men in high places if necessary, or threatening to withdraw all their funds from the Saigon banks.

War refugees account for much of the dramatic rise of Saigon's population. These tragic people began to flood the city in 1959 and their numbers increased rapidly. In 1971 the Ministry for Social Action estimated that they numbered 4,440,000. The refugees are a shifting, uncontrollable population who leave the city during periods of calm in the fighting and return when it escalates. By the end of 1971 many had returned to their villages but the rest remain in Saigon in a perpetual state of anguished waiting. The influx of the peasants to the towns has completely reversed the traditional social and economic structures of Vietnam. From a country which was 85 per cent rural it has become a land where over 40 per cent of the people live in and around towns. The refugees, mostly children, who today number about one million are confronted with unpleasant living conditions. When they arrive they are given about 13 dollars and a pound of rice a day for six months. They have no homes and either live in tents in barbed wire enclosures or in shanty towns thrown together with any available materials such as sheet-iron, planks of wood, cardboard and anything of use salvaged from the rubbish dumps. In order to help support a large family of children whose fathers had been killed or drafted into the army many young girls had no choice but to put aside their traditional moral values and become prostitutes. At the height of the war when American troops were present in their thousands prostitution was the most highly paid profession in Saigon. A prostitute earned more than a university professor. There were nearly one hundred thousand such girls in Saigon and the suburbs. But with the withdrawal of the American troops and their allies has come the inevitable unemployment. The people are thrown back into the misery of shanty town life.

The government of Saigon is now confronted by a huge human problem. Up to now refugees have depended on help from foreign and Vietnamese charity organizations. Great Britain has donated foods, powdered milk and vitamins. Australia has given tents, preserved meat and fish. American organizations have given flour and foodstuffs. The Red Cross, Caritas and the Maltese Order also give aid. Yet it has seemed a bottomless well.

The newest modern problem with which Saigon wrestles is traffic. It is the most chaotic, packed and congested of towns, especially during the rush hour, when large cars, scooters, cyclos, bicycles, motor bikes and people all fight their way along the streets. Almost every other Saigonese seems to be speeding along the streets on his Japanese motor-bike – Saigon is often ironically called 'Honda city'. If a Vietnamese is hoping to spend the profits of his harvest on a motor-bike he will talk of his 'honda rice' and 'honda vegetables'. With all this traffic Saigon has, not unsurprisingly, a high accident rate. In 1970 there were 12,769 accidents – 137 of them fatal. Most of these are caused by peasants and refugees who have just arrived from the country and who tend to be completely ignorant of traffic regulations; or by Saigon youths who roar through the streets, sometimes three to a machine, at breakneck speed.

Today and for centuries Saigon has been the meeting place of the South Vietnamese élite – the politicians, the intelligentsia, the opportunists and the cultured nationalists. Since its beginning as a capital Saigon has never had a truly democratic régime. When the French were in power, a few Vietnamese political parties were formed and all aimed their policies against the foreign colonizers. But these were often driven underground and into silence. It was this more than anything else that led to the emergence of the peasant oriental Communist Party of Indochina and the later birth of the National Liberation Front of South Vietnam.

Since 1967, when the constitution recognized the legal existence of political parties as long as they were neither neutralist nor communist, there has been a resurrection of the old parties and an unprecedented flowering of splinter groups. Although in 1970 fifty groups registered at the Ministry of the Interior in order to obtain legal status there are now only some two dozen political parties or groups active in South Vietnam. The majority of them base their popularity on personal links, friendships and obligations rather than on explicit programs or objectives. Saigon politics give the impression of involving only a few individuals and not the general populace. And the populace tends to distrust all politicians. Membership of all the political parties of Saigon together represent only ten per cent of the population. Weakened as they are by internal divisions and personal ambitions they cannot mobilize the masses. Apart from the National Liberation Front it is only the priests of the various religions – Buddhist, Catholic, Caodaist and Hoa-hoa – who can politically influence the South Vietnamese. Although these religious groups do not have defined political programs, they are important pressure groups, and the success of the political parties depends on their support. In 1970, for example, senator Vu Van Mau, supported by the Buddhists of the Au Quang pagoda – an anti government faction – won 1,148,078 votes, a much higher number than any other of the candidates elected in the Saigon area. The political battle which will determine the future of South Vietnam after thirty years of war will be resolved in Saigon.

The massive involvement of American troops in the war has brought profit to some and poverty to others. The real sufferers of the war are the peasant farmers of South Vietnam. The war has almost completely destroyed the agricultural economy and caused misery, death and unemployment. Japan, Thailand, Taiwan and Singapore have all profited because of the enormous quantities of dollars spent in these countries by American troops on 67

Saigonese South Vietnam

Streets swarm with small
motorcycles, often carrying
three passengers at once.
They have earned Saigon
the nickname 'Honda City'.

leave, and due also to their massive export of manufac-
tured goods, foodstuffs and military equipment which
the Vietnamese needed and which they bought with
American dollars. And in South Vietnam, especially
Saigon, it was the business men, the Chinese and the
urban population in general who profited.

The war has generally favored economic development
in and around Saigon. Formerly North Vietnam was the
most industrialized area while Saigon was, except for a
few small industries—sugar, paper, beer, tobacco and
textile factories—until 1960 essentially the center of
agricultural produce, the rice granary of Vietnam. Since
the war many more industrial firms have been established
in Saigon and the suburb of Giadinh. In 1968 it was
estimated that there were 1,795 firms producing textiles,
foodstuffs and chemicals, indicating a ten per cent
industrial growth rate per year. And Saigon has also been
transformed into a great consumer market for imported
goods – 30 per cent of which come from Japan. Thanks
to American dollars, the people of Saigon have, in
general, known a few years of fabulous wealth. The city
has been overwhelmed by the splendor and proliferation
of western gadgets, of motor cycles, transistors, televisions
and refrigerators.

The protracted war has also left developments which
could be useful to the Vietnamese economy after the
political and military situation has been settled. Vietnam
has two great ports – Haiphong and Saigon. Until 1960
the port of Saigon was a busy center for the export of rice
and rubber from South Vietnam to the countries of
Europe and other parts of the world. During the war the
Americans, besides constructing two new ports – Danang
and Camranh – completely rebuilt, enlarged and
modernized the port of Saigon. It now might well be
considered the biggest port of the Far East, for it is able
to discharge an annual four million tons of cargo.

Air transport has also been rapidly developed over the
last few years. South Vietnam has many more landing
strips than any other country in Asia. Civilian air traffic
has grown by about 25 per cent and the local air line, Air
Vietnam has greatly expanded. To cope with this, Saigon
airport has been enlarged and modernized. And Saigon
is now the center of an excellent network of roads. It can
also boast of computers which deal with electricity, gas
and telephone bills, a magnificent stock of tractors, road
leveling equipment and trucks and an extremely efficient
telecommunications system.

Whether these developments, which could help the
economy of the Saigon region in peacetime, will in fact
do so, depends on their speedy conversion to civilian and
industrial use. The city of Saigon has many favorable
factors for its future growth. It will inevitably constitute
the center of the social and economic development of the
country – a sort of Hong Kong – a commercial pivot for
trade between the countries of South-east Asia and the
rest of the world.

69

Thousands of soldiers made
prostitution Saigon's best
paid profession. A war-time
prostitute could earn more
than a university professor.

People of Cambodia

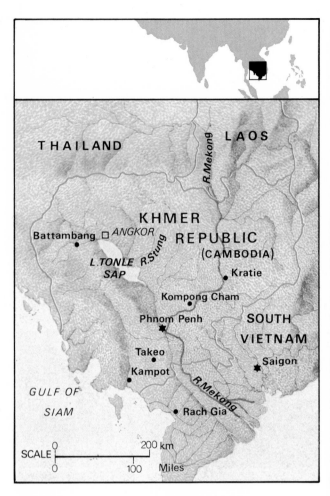

THAILAND

LAOS

R. Mekong

KHMER
REPUBLIC
(CAMBODIA)

ANGKOR

Battambang

L. TONLE
SAP

R. Stung

Kratie

Kompong Cham

Phnom Penh

SOUTH
VIETNAM

Takeo

Saigon

Kampot

GULF OF
SIAM

R. Mekong

Rach Gia

SCALE
0 — 200 km
0 — 100 — Miles

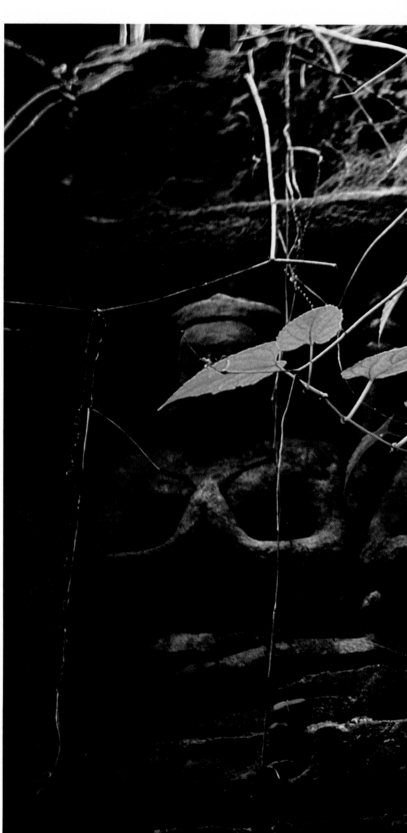

Most of the seven million people in Cambodia are the direct descendants of the Khmer, the people who once ruled the most powerful empire in South-east Asia. The era of this once great civilization, known as the Angkor period, lasted from 802-1432 AD. Its finest remnant, the ancient capital city of Angkor Wat, is one of the greatest wonders of the world.

In its 2,000 years of recorded history Cambodia, the Khmer Republic, has undergone many dramatic changes. The people, who prefer to call themselves Khmer, have known glories, defeats, humiliations, domination and colonization by foreign powers. And throughout all these periods they have encountered the influences of foreign civilizations and religions.

The Cambodian people, especially the peasants who make up 85 per cent of the total population, have certainly been much affected by the present internal strife and the influences resulting from foreign intervention. But their way of life, their values and beliefs, in time of peace at least, have remained much the same as those of their Khmer ancestors. French domination, from 1864

70

Between the 9th and 13th
centuries the Buddhist Khmer
erected the temples and palaces
of Angkor Wat, one of the
greatest wonders of the world.

People of Cambodia

(Bottom) The head of a Naga, a mythical Indian snake, rears majestically from a body supported by a balustrade of 54 stone giants.

Angkor Wat — contemporary with Notre Dame in Paris — was the center of the Khmer people who today occupy the Khmer Republic (Cambodia).

until independence in 1953, tended to influence the ruling élite only, particularly since the gap between the ruling élite and the masses was so great.

The majority of the Khmer today are peasants. Although there are urban Khmer — members of aristocratic families, civil servants and the military — the present-day social system is not entirely dissimilar from that of the 19th century, although some elements of the traditional society have disappeared and new ones have emerged.

Khmer society which is still headed by a monarchy, had in the past a formal hierarchical class system, structured by heredity, with royalty at the top. The upper classes included the nobility — royal descendants more than five generations removed from a sovereign — and the descendants of the Brahmanic priests. The king was an absolute monarch and, as the guardian of the Buddhist religion, in theory owned both his country and his people. Members of the royal family held most of the important civil and military positions and formed the core of the government. Outside the royal aristocracy high social rank depended on royal favor.

The Khmer peasants include the rice growers in the rich flat lands in the south-eastern and north-western parts of the country, especially in the province of Battambang. There are also rice-growers and fishermen around the lake of Tonle Sap, foresters in the hilly regions of the south-west and north-east, sugar palm cultivators in the central part of the country, artisans in the provinces

(Right) Faces of Buddha, in the serenity of deep contemplation, are carved into the rock of the many towers of Bayon Temple.

People of Cambodia

At Siem Reap near Angkor Wat villagers lay peppers on a rack to dry in the sun. Rural life has changed little through the ages.

At Siem Reap near Angkor Wat villagers lay peppers on a rack to dry in the sun. Rural life has changed little through the ages.

of Kandal and Takeo and market gardeners along the fertile banks of the Mekong and Bassac rivers. Practically all other sections of the economy are in the hands of the other ethnic groups, such as the Chinese, who live in Cambodia.

Most of these peasant Khmer live in single houses, built with the help of relatives and neighbors. Their houses are generally rectangular, up to 20 feet wide by 30 feet long with a wooden floor, perched on wood or concrete piles as high as 10 feet off the ground. The height of the floor often depends on the likelihood of flooding during the rainy season, but more often reflects the prosperity of the owner. There is a steeply thatched gabled roof with overhanging eaves to protect the inside from monsoon rains. The matted thatch is of either palm fronds or savanna grass, both of which are used widely throughout South-east Asia. Now houses are being built increasingly of wood, tiles and masonry. The houses are without windows, but a space is left for ventilation between the wall panels and the overhanging eaves. There may be several rooms, separated by partitions of dried palm fronds, but the houses of the poorest peasants often have only a single room. The kitchen is usually a separate room or an adjacent shed, sometimes joined to the house by a ramp. There are few furnishings: only mats, cushions and chests containing one or two garments for each member of the family. Each family has its own statue of Buddha. Festive plates and fruit dishes, which may be either of wood encrusted with mother of pearl or of copper and silver, are always used for entertaining. Bowls of copper and silver are used to serve betel nuts, which figure prominently in most ceremonies.

The Khmer wear traditional clothes in rural areas, but in the towns they turn increasingly to western clothes. The *sampot*, worn by both men and women, is a length of cotton or silk up to ten feet long and three feet wide wrapped around the waist, fastened in front and falling to mid-calf. The top of the remaining material is then passed between the legs and tucked into the waistband in the back. From the front this gives the appearance of loose trousers and, from the back, of a skirt. With the *sampot* women wear a blouse and shawl. For formal occasions men wear a shirt, a high-necked tunic and long socks. In most rural areas children wear a more western form of dress. Boys dress in shorts and shirts, and girls usually wear blouses and skirts.

The Khmer eat much the same food as the Chinese or Vietnamese who live in Cambodia. The typical meal for a peasant family is a ball of rice eaten with the fingers, three dried fish and a bit of *prahoc*: a spicy paste of Cambodian origin made of salted dried fish and allowed to ferment in jars. Rice, fish and water satisfy their basic needs. Rice is not as thoroughly milled as in many other rice countries and is processed less in the rural areas than in the cities. As a result it retains many more vitamins. *Tuk-trey,* a sauce made of fermented, highly

The temple of Ta Prohm is half-stifled by Cambodian jungle. Today it is acting, dancing and music that exemplify Cambodian art.

spiced fish oil is eaten as a staple part of the diet by people of all social levels. For a Cambodian family food at its best is characterized by its mixture of delicate flavors and spices, combining sweet and sour, bland and bitter, in distinctive recipes.

They drink generally between meals, but also present a drink as the first offering to a visitor. To refuse this drink would be considered as rude and unfriendly. They drink water after meals, usually from a large water jug and a common bowl. Supplements to the basic diet depend on both season and on a family's status and wealth. Vegetables, beef and pork, poultry, eggs and fruits, particularly bananas, are all important foods.

The Khmer are cheerful people, in time of peace at least. They have a remarkable sense of humor. They laugh and smile easily. They adore songs and stories and especially festivities. National festivals punctuate the year and bring the people together. In April there is the New Year celebration, in May the Festival of the Sacred Furrows, the Buddhist Festival of Kathen in October, the Festival of the Retreat of Water in November, the king's birthday and the birth and death anniversaries of Buddha and many other religious and secular festivities throughout the year. Despite a sensuality that is revealed in many of their proverbs, tales and songs the Khmer, like most Asians, are also a prudish people. Nudity, for example, always offends them.

The life of a Khmer peasant is regular, in the European sense. It is a monogamous society. (Polygamy once existed in the cities but it is now illegal.) A Khmer woman plays an important role in the family. She almost always has the last word in the household, particularly on matters concerning bringing up children and finances. When a Khmer woman is married, she still retains her maiden name. Young married couples who are not yet fully financially independent live with the parents of the bride and not with those of the groom. The Khmer are affectionate parents who tend to give considerable freedom to their children – which is different in a Vietnamese family for instance.

They are also a pious people. Theravada Buddhism is the state religion and most Khmer practise Buddhism of one form or another. Their piety is apparent in their observance of holy days *(thangay sel)* which generally fall at each quarter of the moon. There are many religious festivities in which practically all the villagers take part. Marriages and funerals are all attended by Buddhist Bikkhus (monks), for the blessing and prayers. They are tolerant of other religions, though only an insignificant number have been converted to other faiths. The Buddhist religion in Cambodia is more than a religion. It is a form of meditation on human suffering and the abolition of this suffering through the dogma of transmigration. In order to escape the successive reincarnation and suffering which accompanies it, it is necessary to detach oneself from all things, in particular from 'self'

A Buddhist initiation ceremony does not tie one to a monastery for life. Many initiates spend only 6 months in the monastery.

75

At the Phnom Penh festival, during the full moon in January, a fakir has slit his tongue with knives to ward off the demons.

(Bottom) In the Mekong river area hopeful peasants pan the shallow river bed for precious stones to supplement their income.

or egotism. It is perhaps because of this conception of life that many economists find the Khmer exasperating when they contemplate a more materialistically based future for them.

Buddhism certainly has great influence on the economy of the country. There are for instance about three thousand Buddhist monasteries in Cambodia. There are nearly 70,000 Bikkhus, although not all of them stay in the monasteries forever. Many become Bikkhus for a short time as a religious duty, especially to show their gratitude to their parents. There are also those who find it necessary to become Bikkhus because in some parts of the country monasteries are the only places to acquire any education. This was certainly true during the period of the French Protectorate. Had there not been Buddhist monasteries, Khmer language and literature might possibly have disappeared long ago. The Bikkhus have always been traditionalist and nationalist and in politics have played important roles. The first resistance to French domination in the 19th century was led by a number of Bikkhus. The same was true during the postwar period. The Bikkhus made a considerable contribution in the Khmer struggle for independence from the French. This is hardly surprising. In the countryside, in every *phum* or village, the monastery is the only place where villagers can have some form of social and religious life. Inevitably it is the center of political consciousness.

Minority groups in Cambodia include the 100,000 Khmer Islam, or Muslim Cambodians, mostly fishermen and artisans who live in two regions in Kampot province in southern Cambodia and along the banks of the Mekong and Tonle Sap rivers. Also called Cham they are the descendants of the people of Champa, a former kingdom of central Vietnam. Another name for them is Chvea, after Malays believed to have first come to Cambodia in the 13th century. The men wear brightly colored sarongs and the women always cover their heads with scarves. All important Khmer Islam villages have a mosque. Many parents still prefer a Koranic education for their children.

The Vietnamese, many of whom are small traders and artisans and who live mostly along the banks of the Mekong and Tonle Sap, are regarded by the Khmer with distrust and animosity. Almost one quarter of them are Roman Catholic, they have retained their distinctive culture, rarely intermarry with the Khmer and are considered aliens in the land. The antipathy is mutual, a legacy of Vietnamese-Khmer history, French colonialism, and French policy of divide and rule. Many Vietnamese were brought to work as clerks in the French administration and were protected by French laws. And Khmer were taken as riflemen to suppress a Vietnamese rebellion against the French. Up to half the 400,000 Vietnamese (in 1970) have been repatriated.

The numbers of the Chinese minority, on the other hand, are difficult to assess because they are well integ-

A boy paddles down through a floating village on the lake of Tonle Sap near Kompong. Fish abound in this great lake of the Mekong river.

(Bottom) The rice fields around Tonle Sap are fertile, and traditional farming methods persist despite the great changes in the cities.

rated in Cambodian society. Since Cambodian independence in 1953 most Chinese have become naturalized Cambodians. Few remain aliens. Certainly the tolerant Buddhism of the country and the long history of amicable relations between China and Cambodia, has contributed to this harmony. Mixed marriages are frequent. Their offspring, often many generations removed, are called Sino-Cambodians. Sino-Cambodians tend to live in the major cities, particularly Phnom Penh, where they play an important economic and financial role and many work in the professions. Although loyal to Cambodia they still retain a distinct Chinese culture, continuing to bury their dead, for example, instead of cremating them, as do most Khmer. They celebrate the Chinese New Year and practise a form of ancestor worship.

The highland minorities, who are officially called Khmer-Loeu meaning Khmer of the highlands or Montagnards, live mostly in north-eastern Cambodia. There are about 300,000 of them and most are both hunters and agriculturalists. The best known minority peoples are the Muong, the Kha and the Jarai.

Among the Europeans who live in Cambodia, the 3,000 French form the largest community. Many are sent by the French government as part of the technical and cultural assistance program. They are university teachers, engineers, military training officers and so on. Then there are those Frenchmen who have lived in Cambodia since the time of the Protectorate. They continue to supervise the French colonial interests, the rubber plantations, banks, insurance and shipping offices. There are also many French people, mostly Corsicans, who own restaurants or bars. Many have been involved in shady businesses like smuggling, black-market dealing and drug trafficking, especially the heroin trade from the 'golden triangle' in northern Laos. They are generally known as the Corsican Mafia of Indochina. In Cambodia also the number of Americans is increasing. Many have been serving as civilian advisors to the present régime in the country.

Before the war started in March 1970 it was commonly accepted that the Cambodians were a happy people. Their social and economic problems were much less pressing than in other developing countries. Land did not belong to landlords as in Vietnam. Khmer peasants, however poor, usually owned their own land. But recently, since the war, many Khmer have become either refugees in Phnom Penh – where there are as many as a million, or have taken to the jungle to join other dissidents. In the cities the Khmer are only now discovering urban problems. Many cannot find work. As for those in the jungle, they have lost their houses, land and livestock. Already there is talk of the power of the masses. And the urban élite faces new demands from these people who were hardly considered before. For now is the first time that any significant number have had contact with each other.

77

Buddhism in South-east Asia

(Above) Building and gilding
temples bring Buddhists
merit. This Mandalay pagoda
is dedicated to the martyred
sons of the holy King, Kanaung.

Religion in South-east Asia is rich in its variety. Islam is dominant in Indonesia, Malaya and Borneo. Christianity has a firm grip on the Philippines. Hinduism has left traces in Indonesia and elsewhere. Confucianism and Taoism live in the minds of the Vietnamese and Chinese who live in this part of the world. Various local forms of animism exist beside the major religions. But above and beyond all these Buddhism is the religion of the majority of people in Burma, Thailand, Cambodia, Laos and Vietnam and also of Sri Lanka (Ceylon).

The cradle of Buddhism is in north-east India, in the basin of the River Ganges. Its origin dates back several centuries before the Christian era. Gautama was the founder of Buddhism, but as he belonged to the Shakya clan he was also later called Shakyamuni (Sage of the Shakya). He was born a prince in the grove of Lumbini, now in Nepal, near Kapilavastu where his father was king. His father provided him with all kinds of pleasures, and tradition tells that he excelled in all learning and arts. It is further said that on four different occasions the prince went out of each of the four gates of the castle and saw first an old man, then a sick man, then a dead man, and lastly a monk. These four visions of the miseries of life and of the peace to be obtained in the religious life made him reflect deeply on the meaning of existence. One night at the age of 29 (or 19 according to other traditions) he left the palace and set out to seek the way. He visited two great spiritual teachers of the time, and after that he followed extreme ascetic practices, but all to no avail. Finally he took to meditating in a cross-legged posture. In his deep meditation he attained perfect serenity of mind. In this serenity he realized omniscience and awakened to ultimate truth. And so he became Buddha, 'the Enlightened One', when he was 35 years old.

The rest of his life was dedicated to the dissemination of Dharma, 'the law', as his teaching was called. He made converts among his friends, kings, merchants, and others from all walks of life, and so the community of monks, called Sangha, continued to grow. In his wanderings he taught many people, and sent out his followers on missionary activities. At the age of 80 he passed away at Kushinagara, the modern Kasia. According to the tradition popular in South-east Asia he died in 544 BC, but modern scholars estimate that it was in either 486 or 383 BC.

Since his time Buddhism has spread far and wide, throughout Asia and even beyond. Throughout its history Buddhism has never used force to impose its

faith or extend its frontiers and it has always adapted itself quickly to different situations. It was tolerant of other ways of thinking and incorporated aspects of other beliefs in its system. As Buddhism grew to maturity in India many Hindu deities were absorbed into its pantheon. In Tibet it incorporated many Bon elements into its mystic system of Tantrism. Ch'an (or Zen) Buddhism developed out of its contact with Taoism in China. In Japan Buddhism has generally co-existed happily with the native religion of Shintoism, absorbing some of the Shinto deities.

In South-east Asia local beliefs have been similarly assimilated. In Sri Lanka even devil dancing and the practice of thread-tying are performed as if they were an essential part of Buddhist practice. Thread-tying is a ceremony in which monks chant scriptures while all hold a thread connected to a window or something else through the hand of an image of Buddha. In Burma the native worship of animistic spirits called *nats* exists alongside Buddhism. Images of *nats* are placed in Buddhist temples and pagodas. In Thailand new homes, for example, are blessed by the ceremony of thread-tying. Further, the grand temple of Angkor Wat of Cambodia bears witness to a happy mixture of the native animism, Hinduism and Buddhism.

Buddhism has planted the belief in Karma and Retribution deep in the minds of the South-east Asians. Belief in Karma promises a better, happier future by the performance of good, meritorious acts in this life, whereas evil acts will bring about miserable retribution in the next life. Sufferings in hell are often depicted frightfully and fearfully on the walls of Thai temples where they serve to remind visitors of the great pains that await sinners. For laymen the cardinal virtue is to observe the Five Precepts that is to say: not killing, not stealing, not committing adultery, not lying, and not drinking. But giving gifts to the Sangha, offering food to monks, repairing temples and participating in Buddhist ceremonies are all considered meritorious acts. Furthermore in order to gain merit, people often free captured fish and stick gold leaves on the Buddha's image. In Burma the construction of new pagodas is considered the most meritorious act. It is said that repairing an old pagoda gains one little merit unless one is a descendant of the original builder.

In Buddhism six states of transmigratory existence are distinguished. From the lowest level to the highest they are hell, hungry ghosts, animals, fighting spirits, men and heavenly beings. Most people engaged in merit-winning acts seek to secure happiness and pleasure in the next life, whether to be born again into the human world or into the heavenly world. Some of them may wish to become rich and live in luxury rather than attain happiness in spiritual terms. These six states of existence lie, after all, in the shadow of suffering caused by spiritual darkness and egoistic desire. But the primary

79

For this woman, meditation and spiritual transcendence beyond the senses can lead to Nirvana, perpetual enlightenment, where the cycle of rebirth is ended.

Other Buddhas—'enlightened ones'—probably preceded Gautama Buddha, of the Ganges basin (born 563BC), whose image presides at Myatmuni.

aim of Buddhism is to attain a state called Nirvana, which means literally extinction, a state which transcends the other six states and so liberates the individual from the cycle of rebirth. Nirvana is the state of the total extinction of passions and is the highest spiritual bliss.

All Buddhist teachings center on Nirvana, and all the various precepts and practices are directed towards the attainment of this goal. The monks are supposed to devote themselves to this every waking moment. They have 227 precepts to observe and have to lead a monastic life well apart from the secular world. They are dependent on alms giving, always being careful of their conduct, which must be sincere and meditative.

Some time after the Buddha's death the Sangha split into two. One group held the spoken words of the Buddha to be the absolute authority, while the other took a more open-minded attitude and contended that what he meant was more important than what he said. Schism followed schism until there were 18 schools. Of these 18 schools the Theravada, 'the School of the Elders', which is based on the verbal teaching of the Buddha, has become the prevailing form of Buddhism in Sri Lanka, Burma, Thailand, Laos and Cambodia. Theravada uses scriptures in Pali, the sacred language which it claims was used by the Buddha.

Some time around the 1st century BC a new movement arose inside Buddhism which claimed to be the true successor of Dharma 'the Law'. It had a new lofty ideal of the Bodhisattva, 'being of enlightenment', and styled itself as Mahayana, 'the Great Vehicle', as distinct from the traditional schools which it called Minayana, 'the Small Vehicle'. Mahayana was transmitted to central Asia, China, Tibet and other areas of the Far East. In South-east Asia the only country where Mahayana still prevails is Vietnam, where a Chinese form of it is practised, a mixture of Ch'an meditation and the worship of Amitabba, the Buddha of Infinite Light who dwells in the Western Paradise.

According to tradition the Buddha visited Sri Lanka to spread the Dharma, leaving his 'footprint' on the top of a mountain, now thought to be the mountain called Adam's Peak. From the historical point of view, however, Buddhism was first introduced into Sri Lanka in the middle of the 3rd century BC by a group of monks led by Mahinda, the son of King Ashoka. The form of Buddhism they brought to Sri Lanka was the one called Theravada. Under royal patronage it soon became the dominant religion of the island. And it was in Sri Lanka that, about the beginning of the Christian era, the sacred teachings, which had up till then been transmitted orally, were written down for the first time in the Pali language.

In the middle of the 11th century, Theravada was first transmitted to Burma from Sri Lanka. At that time there was already in that country a form of Buddhism as well as local beliefs and Hinduism, but all were overshadowed

Monks wander the streets of Bangkok with alms bowls. Those who offer them gifts increase their merit and hopes of a higher state in the next world.

At Wat Po cloistered rows of Buddhas watch over men who may have adopted the life and disciplines of a monk for a few months or a lifetime.

In Old Bangkok a monk walks down a street careful not to harm a living creature. Some strain their drinking water for fear of eating insects.

by this Sinhalese form of Theravada. When, later, Buddhism declined in Sri Lanka Burmese monks were invited to help revive it.

Thai Buddhism, dominated by Theravada, began to flourish in the 14th century after the king had invited some monks from Sri Lanka. Ever since then it has thrived as the state religion. Thailand was once part of the Khmer empire of Cambodia in which Buddhism, Theravada and also Mahayana (transmitted from India around the 5th century) flourished side by side with Hinduism and the native animism. When the territory of this empire was reduced to about the present size of Cambodia by Thai inroads from the 14th century on, the Sinhalese form of Theravada came to supplant all other forms of religion.

During the period of western colonization Buddhism had a difficult time. Under foreign influence Buddhism in Sri Lanka declined again in the 18th century, but then Theravada was once more re-imported into the island from Burma and Thailand. Penetration by Christianity was an inevitable concomitant of western colonialism, and the Catholic Church has been a power in Vietnam since the time of French colonialism. Christian missionaries have converted some minorities in Burma. The kind of Christianity which is linked to English education

has spread in Sri Lanka since the advent of British rule.

Today Buddhism is the state religion of Thailand and Cambodia. The Thai constitution even goes so far as to stipulate that the king has to be a Buddhist and a protector of the Dharma. In Burma although, officially, all religions may be freely practised, Buddhism has long been the unifying force in the country.

Today in Thailand and Burma most education is expounded in the temples. In Cambodia in recent years the expansion of educational facilities connected with Buddhism has represented an attempt to keep this traditional role of the temples in step with the modern world. The practice of spending a period of one's life in the Sangha is still carried on in Thailand and Burma, and it sometimes happens that those whose intention was to live among the monks for no more than three months have gone on living with them for thirty years or more. People are free to join and leave the Sangha. Returning to the secular world does not imply any failure. The experience of a monk's life gives a man a good basis in society all through life.

Recent political and social changes in South-east Asia have inevitably affected the people's Buddhist way of life, but Buddhism still maintains its identity. For most it is the conscience and the principle of behavior in their secular, no less than in their spiritual, lives.

Women light candles—but rarely follow the 'eightfold path'. In Sikkim wives share monastery life platonically with husbands whose children they once bore.

People of Thailand

A strong Theravada Buddhist
faith binds the Thai to each
other and to temples like
Wat Phra Keo, the temple
of the emerald Buddha.

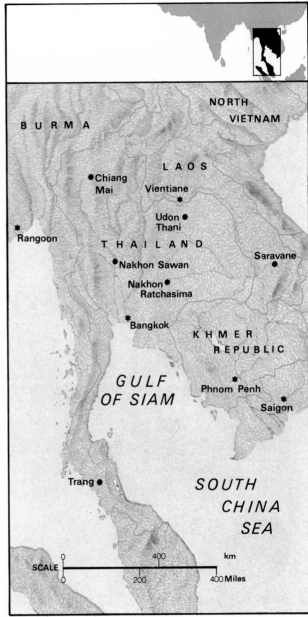

The Kingdom of Thailand is probably still better known by its old name Siam. It is really too little known at all considering its size and importance. For it is a country the size of France with a population of some 35 millions. It lies in the very heart of South-east Asia and its capital, Bangkok, a city of 3 million inhabitants is an international crossroads. Few international travelers go far beyond the lures of this metropolis, but those who wish to understand this country and its peoples must travel out to its district regions and make acquaintance with the villagers who form well over 80 per cent of the population.

If we start in the south we are in a Malay world. Here there are a million Malay speaking, mostly Muslim

People of Thailand

Fawn Lep, the fingernail dance
performed by princesses in
the palaces of northern kings
at Chiang Mai, was for a long
time forbidden to commoners.

Together with plows and
seed, an ox is brought to the
king to be blessed at the
plowing ceremony to
ensure a good crop.

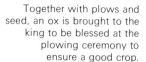

people. We find small-scale rubber planters, and rich tin mining areas as in Malaya. Since we are on a peninsula there are many fishing villages on the coast. Further north, past the narrow Kra isthmus, we come up against the mountain range which divides Thailand from Burma. This is the home of the Karen people. The lack of roads makes it a more impenetrable barrier for the modern traveler than for conquering armies of Thai and Burmese in the past. Skirting Bangkok we arrive in the great central plain of the Chao Phraya river; the plain is flat as far as the eye can see. Most of the trees have been cut down to make more rice fields though over one hundred years ago it was thickly forested. Here transport is mostly along the network of streams and canals. Children go to school by boat; monks make their daily rounds by boat; and, most important, rice reaches the market by boat. The Thai of the central plain are the Siamese proper, heirs to the traditions of the Siamese state of the Ayuthaya period (1350-1767 AD).

To the north-east, on the Korat plateau and beyond, lies a less fertile land with unpredictable rainfall and flooding and consequently a poorer region. Here live nearly one third of the population of Thailand who are more properly called Lao. In the past they have owed allegiance both to Laotian and to Siamese kingdoms. They have a tradition of independence, even opposition, to central government. Their cousins in the north of Thailand were formerly even more independent. Theirs was the kingdom of Chiengmai until 1874 when the Siamese changed a rather tenuous tribute relationship into one of direct administration. These Thai-Yuan have a distinct language and culture. They also live in a different, rather wilder environment, in smallish upland valleys surrounded by thickly forested hills which are inhabited by neighbors of many different ethnic groups: Akha, Karen (see pages 126-129), Lahu, Lisu, Lua (see pages 122-125), Meo (see pages 92-97) and Yao (see pages 46-49). Their regional capital, Chiengmai, is the second city of Thailand, with a population of almost 100,000.

All these Thai peoples, together with the Shan (see

84

Bangkok lies spread out before
Wat Saket, the Temple of the
Golden Mount, built on a
man-made mountain at the
request of a Chiang Mai king.

The fields are rolled after plowing. Thailand depends almost entirely on rice; three out of four of its people grow or sell it.

pages 130-135) and the Lao, and the Tai hill people of northern Vietnam (see pages 24-39), belong to the same language group, with as much variety as the Romance languages of Europe. There are also two other, less numerous, groups of Tai languages whose speakers live in northern Vietnam and southern China. These Thai are relative latecomers in the history of the immigration of peoples and cultures in South-east Asia. We hear little of them until about the beginning of the second millennium AD. Some Thai were no doubt living to the south as subordinate members of the Khmer empire which extended north, at least as far as Chiengmai. It is not until about 1253 AD when the armies of Kublai Khan overthrew what was possibly a part Thai kingdom, Nanchao in Yunnan, that we begin to find small Thai chiefdoms, then kingdoms, coming into their own. We have an early European source of information for this period in the stories of Marco Polo who visited the devastated area of Nanchao some thirty years after its fall and recorded many cultural details still typical of the Thai-Yuan: the eating of *laap,* or chopped and seasoned raw pork; tattooing; ancestor worship; the exorcism of spirits to heal the sick; and the extravagant polygamy of chiefs.

Two famous kings of this period—Mangrai, King of Lannathai (Chiengmai) and Rama Khamheng, King of Sukhothai—have passed into legend as culture heroes, and Mangrai at least is still worshipped as a powerful spirit. They were said to have formed a political alliance by drinking each other's blood; a pact still taken to symbolize the unity of Thai peoples. As Thai history books tell us, the direct line of descent to the modern Thai monarchy passes through Rama Khamheng. A stone inscription of 1292 AD made by this king is something like the Magna Carta of the Siamese. The land abundantly provides: 'In the water there are fish, in the fields there is rice'. The king guaranteed mercy, generosity and access to all his people. It would be a mistake however to regard this style of kingship as characteristic of the later kingdom of Ayuthaya, which developed from the middle of the 14th century as the Khmer empire waned, and lasted until the Burmese sacked the city of Ayuthaya in 1767 AD.

The more progressive kings of Ayuthaya gave the Thai a body of laws and forms of administration from which we can learn much to help us understand even contemporary Thailand. This is so because Thailand's political evolution has known neither revolutionary changes nor direct colonial rule. For instance very early on the older system of hereditary territorial chiefs or princes gave way to a more centralized, bureaucratic one, in which royalty, aristocracy and other nobles were given offices, posts and ranks which could be recalled or forfeited. There was little or no distinction between civil and military posts – a feature that lingers on, as also does the once more highly organized, hierarchical system of patron-client relationships.

The whole population, except the king whose worth 85

People of Thailand

Gas stations stand beside the
canals for motorized sampans
in Bangkok, often called the
Venice of the East
because of its many canals.

86

Rains and fasting have ended
and the king sails down the
Menam river for *Tot Kathin*,
the presentation of new
robes to monks at Wat Po.

Pre-Buddhist beliefs still draw the childless to this phallic shrine where they pray for fertility and ancient rites are conducted.

(Bottom) Food market in Bangkok: a delicacy among the hill Thai is live monkey brain – the skull is sawn open and the brain scooped out.

was inestimable, was ranked and classified by a system known as *sakdina*. This was measured, symbolically at least, in terms of entitlement to land. The viceroy was ranked at 100,000; all those of 400 and above were appointed by the king and drank an annual oath of loyalty. They were entitled to a certain number of freeman clients who mostly had a rank of between 10 and 25. Slaves, of whom there were many kinds, beggars and paupers had a rank of five or less. Depending on how close they lived to their patron, clients would give either their labor directly, or local, usually rare, produce as tribute to their lord.

By far the most dramatic institution was that of kingship itself. According to the fullest interpretation of the ideology of divine kingship, derived from India via the Khmer with later Buddhist additions, the king was an incarnation of the highest divine powers, of Siva and Vishnu, and of India the world ruler; also guardian of the Buddhist law, and even a Boddhisattva or future Buddha. In short he was supremely sacred. His person, throne, palace, capital city, in fact the ideal structure of the whole kingdom had symbolic and magic meanings. After his coronation the king processed in pomp, clockwise round the city on his sacred albino elephant, symbolizing the sun's progress – as was thought – round the earth. Human and cosmic order were inter-dependent. The king presided over annual rites to ensure the rise and fall of the waters, and the success of the crops.

Unlike King Rama Khamheng, the king of Ayuthaya was remote and hedged with taboos in his palace, surrounded by mercenary bodyguards, Portuguese musketeers (after 1511 AD), Persians, Japanese and others. When he left his palace on rare occasions the people were prohibited from even looking at him from behind the fences they had to build along his path, on pain of being shot at by a bodyguard. These kings did pay tribute to the emperor of China, but regarded themselves as equals of such other 'divine' kings as James I of England and Louis XIV of France with whom they exchanged gifts and embassies.

The kingdom of Siam was virtually closed to western contact for about 150 years until well into the 19th century. By this time the capital had moved to Bangkok. At the end of the 19th century King Chulalongkorn, Siam's most progressive monarch, initiated many modernizing trends and successfully kept the French and British at bay, though they did succeed in nibbling away large tracts of territory which became parts of Burma, Malaya, Laos and Cambodia. In 1932 a coup d'état, the first of many, established a constitutional monarchy, which still retains many of the trappings of former times.

One of the dominant characteristics of Asian societies is the relative independence of village communities. Kingdoms might rise and fall; rulers might be more or less oppressive; but the patterns of village life changed more slowly, if at all. Travelers to the villages leave

87

Many Thai have adopted western dress but they cling to Buddhism which not only sanctifies their marriages, but dominates their whole lives.

behind court pageantry, electrified cities and surfaced roads. Whether paddling up a small canal or bumping along in a bullock cart, now through choking dust, now axle-deep in mud, the village at the end of the slow journey will be much the same as any other despite local dialects and customs.

In the middle of flat, wet rice fields, we will see a cluster of trees: tall coconut palms if the village is a hundred years old or more, wide banana leaves, sugar and areca (betel) nut; palms and bamboo thickets. Partly hidden among these trees are the fenced compounds of villagers' houses. There are small boys of seven or eight tending their precious water buffalo; women and girls fishing with shrimp nets, and perhaps men coming from the forest with home-made muzzle-loaders on their shoulders. At the height of the agricultural season, we will see large groups of fifty or more men and women of all ages helping each other planting or harvesting the rice.

As we go closer we are sure to discover the gracefully sloping roof, with carved and colored gables, of the village temple, and hear the wind bells hanging from its eaves. Friendly villagers will ask us politely and softly with a smile: 'Where are you going?' 'Where have you come from?' 'Have you eaten yet?' We will be invited into one of the wooden houses built of light bamboo if a poorer villager, or the handsome solid teak house if a rich peasant; up three or five or seven steps – odd numbers to keep unwanted spirits out. Outside the secure area of homes and fields is an uncertain, possibly hostile world of forest spirits and wild animals. Whether our host is rich or poor we will be offered cool water from an earthenware pot, betel nut to chew, or home grown tobacco. We will sit on the floor, on mats brought out to show respect for visitors.

Thai people have a highly developed and delicate etiquette both of language and body movement. Men sit neatly cross-legged, women sideways on their haunches; both taking care not to expose their feet, which are always kept bare inside the house. It is very improper to stand or sit higher than respected guests, or to offer anything except with a bow and both hands extended. The language has many terms to indicate respect, a quite different set of terms for speaking to monks, and another for royalty. Nobody can keep up such formality for ever. We should not be surprised to find that the language also allows much punning and word play, often bawdy. For instance courtship is a mixture of physical prudery and subtle verbal lewdness. Not even hands will touch – except when the old people are not looking, or in the fields at harvest time. . . . At New Year the wildest behavior is permitted: even monks may have mud thrown at them, women go singing in tipsy processions, and the young men engage in semi-ritualized brawls with those of other villages.

The Thai house may look simple enough, but it is

Often seen at temple fairs, a bout of Thai boxing starts with a prayer. Boxers use feet, elbows, fists, knees, in fact everything but teeth.

invested with many symbolic meanings. These are associated with the birth, marriage and death of its members, and with guardian and ancestral spirits who are kept informed and asked for help on all important occasions. Various thresholds, relative heights of different parts, and compass directions of the layout of the house are all given social significance. A young suitor may not step into the bedroom; the father must sleep in the north-east corner on the right of his wife; the dead may only leave by a certain door; men with magical powers will never step underneath the raised house for fear of ritual pollution from the presence of women overhead. Elaborate ceremonies are conducted when the house-posts are first set up, asking permission from the *nagas*, the giant snakes or dragons who have their kingdom below the earth. Further ceremonies are held when the new house is first entered. This is often an occasion, as are other religious events, for a public display of wealth. Rich peasants may rebuild their houses more often than really necessary in order to gain prestige in the eyes of their neighbors.

The largest part of a villager's surplus wealth – as much as a quarter of his total annual production, is spent on the village temple and the novices and monks who live in it. The temple does not belong to the monks; it is communal property. It is a storehouse of all that is most sacred: the image of the Buddha, the sacred texts which ordained men learn to read and write, musical instruments which they play: gongs, drums, cymbals and reed flutes. Most novices, ordained at about 12 years old, and monks, ordained at 20 or older, only temporarily renounce the world of the family and economic activity. When they disrobe, in their own time, they acquire a title of ex-novice or ex-monk, and will probably become the secular leaders of the community in later life. About half the men of any village will have had some temple experience, however short. They are not then a class or caste apart, but the sons, nephews and grandsons of other villagers. Parents make great merit by sponsoring an ordination ceremony. Next to the series of funeral 89

A bamboo rocket is prepared
for launching. Noisy
festivities drive evil
spirits away with spectacular
rocket displays and balloons.

Silkworm cocoons are dropped
into boiling water to
prevent the thread sticking.
Each cocoon yields up
to two miles of thread.

Krebee Krabong means 'stick
and staff'. Thai are peaceful
people, but they enjoy
performances of the classical
art of self-defense.

Only 70 per cent of
Thai are literate and
this Bangkok Chinese
calligrapher has a small
sideline in letter writing.

(Bottom) A silversmith
in Chiang Mai, Thailand's
great northern center,
concentrates on the intricate
design of an offering bowl.

ceremonies, ordination is the most lavish, striking, and the most charged with social and metaphysical meaning. In the ordination ceremony which is a kind of initiation for young men, the candidate undergoes a symbolic death at the hands of his elders. He must fast, be secluded, shave his hair, beard and eyebrows, remain celibate and renounce other worldly pleasures. Yet he is no sooner robed in yellow than his elders prostrate themselves before him and ask him for blessings and the recitation of sacred law. This exchange between young and old is reversed at death and after. Then it is the turn of the young, especially the young monks, to care for their elders, their parents, grandparents, aunts and uncles. The young must ensure their safe passage to the world of spirits and their progress towards rebirth with improved status in the world of men.

This subordination of younger to older generations, and within a generation of younger to older brothers and sisters, is one of the main principles of social organization among the Thai. For the Thai peoples, in common with Burmese, Cambodian and Lao peasants, do not have large-scale clans or descent groups. Their kinship system is known as 'bilateral'; that is with equal stress on the mother's side and father's side, and with little genealogical depth.

The small family household is the chief unit of production and consumption of basic necessities. Married children will spend a few years living with their parents and helping in the fields. Usually the new son-in-law will go to live with his wife's family, performing a kind of bride service. When his wife's younger sister marries he will leave with his wife to set up his own house not far away. The household cannot however provide all the labor it needs for the more intensive agricultural tasks. For these it relies on kinsmen and neighbors, and on a tradition of co-operative exchange of labor for labor. These co-operative relationships and alliances have to be carefully maintained. Invitations must be sent out to attend funerals, ordination, housewarmings and the like.

In addition to these alliances the community as a whole has common interests and concerns. The community needs to co-operate to maintain the system of irrigation dams and canals, village paths, cart-tracks, bridges, and wayside shelters. There is the costly upkeep of the temple, and participation in the temple rituals which mark the distinct Buddhist and agricultural lunar calendars. The community also needs spiritual help of a practical kind which Buddhism cannot strictly provide. Hence there are cults and shrines for local guardian spirits; often these are long dead heroes and princes. There is a series of rites to exorcise or ward off evil influences. Among these are the spectacular launching of explosive rockets, hot-air balloons, and large decorated rafts floated down rivers. All these serve a magic purpose as well as providing much fun and gaiety which all Thai people like to engage in.

In common with peasant peoples the world over the Thai are more and more drawn into national and international political and economic systems. The town market and the district office are increasingly familiar institutions. Central government officials, dressed in khaki uniforms, caps and badges, whether military men or civilian teachers, involve themselves in village life, sometimes well-intentioned and effective, sometimes haughty, corrupt and distanced from the rural people. Village land, once free for all, becomes scarcer and passes into the hands of fewer people. Urban interests extend into the country. The phenomenon of landless peasants and under- or unemployed urban slum dwellers appear. In some areas this gives rise to dissidence and opposition. There is a sense however in which the Thai people are united in their shared culture, their Buddhist religion, and respect for monarchy. Thai rulers too are unlikely to depart for long from their traditional and skilful diplomatic policies of cautious alliances, and pragmatic friendships with all powerful neighbors. In any case the interests and resources of the largest and ultimately most powerful part of the nation cannot for long be ignored – the Thai peasant farmers whose social lives and customs we have glimpsed in these pages.

91

Meo
Vietnam, Laos, Thailand & Burma

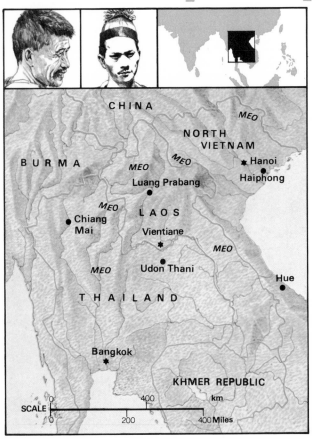

During the first Indochina war in the 1860s common soldiers and officers of the French Expeditionary Force were said to be so fascinated by the way of life of the Hmong, as the Meo of South-east Asia are called, that they had no wish ever to return home. Through their subsistence economy, which supplies them with the necessities with which they so successfully survive, the Hmong seem to have gained all the treasures and leisures which seem to elude economically complex western 20th century consumer society.

Throughout their history the Hmong have been distinguished by their great love of independence. Whenever this has been threatened – as has frequently happened – they have tended to retreat to inaccessible places rather than submit. This has been possible because their material culture allows them an independent economic existence so even today, as they are sustained by subsistence farming they may isolate themselves from all contact with the outside world. As well as being a farmer and as well as growing opium to sell, each man is also his own blacksmith, jeweler and carpenter and every woman is a weaver and tailor.

Come what may, their culture and the structure of their extremely fragmented society can always re-establish itself in small pockets and there flourish.

93

The Meo are peaceful farmers,
but conflicts throughout
their troubled history have
pushed them into ever more
isolated mountain areas.

Wherever the Hmong settle they re-establish themselves into clans whose members trace their ancestry through the male line. Their villages rarely contain more than ten households – all belonging to the same lineage. In fact the lineage and the village are one and the same thing, and the head of the lineage is also the head of the village. Internal disputes are settled by an assembly of the heads of households. No important decision can be taken without the consent of all the senior men concerned. These assemblies also choose members to represent them to the national administration.

Clan members must marry outside their own clan, so the villages form alliances with each other. If a village group is decimated by an epidemic the survivors will seek out others of their lineage to whom they may attach themselves. A new lineage may even emerge from the association of strangers who share the same clan name, and therefore consider themselves brothers.

The household, called the *i che neng,* is under the strict control of the head of the family, the *tucheu che.* Members of a household, although linked by kinship, are not bound by it. Married brothers and sons sometimes leave the household to escape the authority of an elder brother or father. They must, however, build their own house and become fully responsible for all the needs of their own family. They may either stay in the village and within the lineage or settle in the forest or in another village.

Their wooden houses are built directly on the ground, although their storage lofts are raised on piles. The houses each have two doors, but no windows or chimneys, and two fireplaces – one to cook on and one as a hearth. Each group within the extended family has its own sleeping platform. The houses are rather roughly built because they are only temporary: the Hmong move on to new ground every few decades.

The Hmong like to establish large households. The bigger the household, the bigger the source of labor to clear fields from the forest. Isolated couples know they may suffer several years of hardship while their children are too young to work. Polygamy frequently solves the problem – if the husband can afford a second bride-price. At every marriage a large sum of money is paid to the bride's parents. As this must be returned if a woman wishes to separate from her husband, divorce is rare. Unhappy wives are left with the choice of simply fleeing the village or committing suicide, leaving the husband with the burden of paying damages ('the price of the head') to the wife's parents.

As marriage between people of the same clan is strictly forbidden the partners are always from different villages.

The most important crop grown by the Meo is opium. Poppies are always planted in the best fields — here, at Bong Hai, in the middle of the village.

94

In November, poppies are in full bloom but they are no use to the Meo until January when the petals have fallen from the resinous seed pod.

With a special three-bladed knife a Meo man makes three parallel scratches in the seed pod to allow the opium resin to ooze out.

(Bottom) At first the sap is white, but by the time it is scraped off the pod, the day after cutting, it is beginning to turn black.

Before marriage girls have plenty of freedom. They may be courted in the fields or at home. The bride-price is fixed with the aid of go-betweens after discussions between the families. If a boy is afraid of being unacceptable to the bride's parents he may persuade the girl to elope with him. After that they return to open negotiations with the advantage of a *fait accompli*. The new bride goes to live in her father-in-law's house in a nearby village.

The Hmong women wear turbans – elaborately wound for special occasions – and shave the front of their heads clean, so that no hair shows. The men have abandoned traditional clothing, but still wear silver jewelry to keep up their social prestige. All the unmarried girls' spare time is devoted to the intricate embroidery of the festive costumes which they wear at marriage feasts and other festivals. The most important festival is the New Year in February, when there is little work to be done and the villages buzz with the sound of singing and flutes, and when young maidens decked out in silver jewelry throw balls back and forth with the boys of their choice, talking and singing of love.

Except for these days of gaiety and extravagant feasting the year is devoted to the different tasks of the *ray*: the staggered cultivation of rice, maize and of opium, the Hmong's main source of cash. A stretch of forest is axed down and vegetation left to dry and then burned. The earth, fertilized with the ashes, is planted at the first rains. Opium is cultivated by the women after the men have put up a woven bamboo fence around the plot. Hmong households use little opium themselves but grow it principally to sell. They invest the surplus cash in silver jewelry and silver bars. The Hmong also hunt, grow vegetables and keep livestock. Almost every household owns a cossetted horse – as much for prestige as for use.

Chinese culture has strongly influenced not only their material culture but also their religious beliefs. Some of their household deities, for example, are obviously Chinese: the Fourth Mandarin (the Spirit of Wealth) the Jade Emperor (the Spirit of Medicine), and the Guardian

95

Fresh opium sap is scraped off the poppy pods with a knife. After a few days, when it has turned black it will be sold for $40 a kilo.

A refugee in Lao Teung prepares a small ball of opium for smoking by heating and rolling it into shape to fit into his pipe.

of the Front Door; while the Spirits of the Bedroom, the Central Pillar and the Fireplace are uniquely Hmong.

There are also ceremonies, such as the Quest of the Souls, where the archaic Hmong character is mixed with certain elements of Chinese Taoism. The shaman's troop of soldiers (his auxiliary spirits), for example, who accompany him on the Path of the Beyond during his hunt for the fugitive souls, are partly Chinese. He addresses them in the Chinese language, speaking Hmong to the others. In the same way the exorcisms spoken by blacksmiths and shamans use magic formulae (*kaeu kong*) inherited from popular Taoism.

Funeral rites and beliefs about death are more authentically Hmong. The corpse is kept in the house as long as possible – anything from three days to almost three weeks – and carefully watched over. While the long funeral rites and involved sacrifices are being carried out, the house is filled with the sound of a drum and the *kr'eng* (a six-tubed bamboo pipe) which guides the soul on its way. At the beginning of the ceremonies a singer initiates the soul in the origins of the world, man, death and disease. The final part of this epic song guides the soul on the route away from this earth, through the sky, helping it to overcome the obstacles met on the way, until it reaches the village of the ancestors, where it will find the means to reincarnation.

The Hmong believe that they are descendants of an incestuous brother and sister, the sole human survivors of the Great Flood – a myth of origin shared with the Chinese, who call the brother and sister Fu Hsi and Nu Wa.

They are in fact, with the Hmu and the Kho Siong, one of an ancient group of three distinct but related Meo tribes, known traditionally by the Chinese as the Miao. One third – about 550,000 – of the total Hmong population lives in the neighboring countries of North Vietnam, Laos, Thailand and Burma; 1,129,000 live in the southern Chinese provinces of Kweichow, Szechuan, Kuangsi, and Yunnan.

In the mythical times of the Legendary Emperors (2,852-2,255 BC) Chinese books mention a fierce tribe called the San Miao (the Three Miao), who revolted against the Chinese founder heroes and who were repressed by such great characters as Emperor Shun and Yu the Great. Abundant controversies, as yet unresolved, have divided scholars and sinologists on the question of whether to accept that the historical Miao are descendants of these proto-historical San Miao. There is however considerable evidence to suggest that this is so.

History records that the Miao continued their resistance to the Chinese Empire and succeeded in preserving their archaic non-literate culture. But they revolted regularly, provoked Chinese repression and were driven gradually southwards into remote, inhospitable mountainous areas. These revolts were evidently often inspired by a messianic belief which recurs among the Meo, that they would be granted a

New Year is a great festival for the Meo. Young people play ball games while men sit in the shade playing the *naw*, a bamboo wind instrument.

An intricate pattern is worked on a length of cloth by batik, a complicated process using dye and wax, found all over Asia.

supernatural king, and their own writing system. This king would enable them to establish their own administration, free from Chinese domination. Their last great rebellions under the Manchu dynasty in the late 19th century were cruelly crushed. As a result there was a massive migration of Hmong rebels group from Kweichow and Kuangsi into Yunnan and northern Indochina.

Since then the Hmong have spread peacefully in the mountainous areas of North Vietnam, Laos, Thailand and Burma. The messianic phenomenon is still alive among these scattered people. In their new homelands messianic movements have continued to appear from time to time. The most violent of all these manifestations, the Pachai Revolt (or, as the Hmong call it, the War of the Madman), engulfed the whole of northern Indochina, from Dien Bien Phu to Luang Prabang, from 1918 to 1921. The French colonial administration rigorously suppressed the revolt and, after years of fleeing from the swift patrols which the French sent out to track him down, Pachai was finally murdered. Considered by some to be a madman, to others he quickly became a legendary figure and in North Vietnam and North Laos today his name is a symbol of the Hmong struggle for political recognition.

After a period of calm between the two world wars their history receded into the background as the Hmong began to feel the reverberations of the conflicts which shook the modern world. During the Japanese invasion and later the wars of Indochina, the Hmong took up arms on both sides and gained access to the military and administrative hierarchies in the camps where they fought. Unfortunately the assimilation which some of them achieved in this way cost many lives and resulted in massive movements of Hmong into refugee camps.

The Chinese People's Republic and the Democratic Republic of North Vietnam have in recent years adopted a policy of integrating their ethnic minorities. This includes literacy campaigns and the introduction of cadres, school teachers and medical teams. The old and the new élites were granted a measure of administrative autonomy to interest them in the changes. Lack of information and particularly of eye-witness reports makes it difficult to ascertain what has now happened to the Hmong as a separate group in these countries. But it is possible to assess their numbers and their whereabouts fairly accurately from census figures and linguistic research carried out before the literacy campaigns.

In Thailand, a haven of calm and a refuge for those who fled the wars in Laos and Burma, there were from 1968 onwards repeated clashes with tactless local civil servants which provoked several thousand Hmong into resistance to the Thai government. The Thai army intervened but pockets of dissidence remain to this day, maintained by the villagers who are organized by their guerilla leaders. Fortunately the rugged terrain and poor communications mean that in Laos, Thailand and Burma it is still possible for other pockets of Hmong to live in peace. Entrenched in the mountains these Hmong groups are determined, against all odds, to preserve their culture and harmonious existence as slash-and-burn farmers. **97**

People of Burma

The future of this dead man's soul depends on whether the correct funeral rituals are observed, as well as on the good he has done in life.

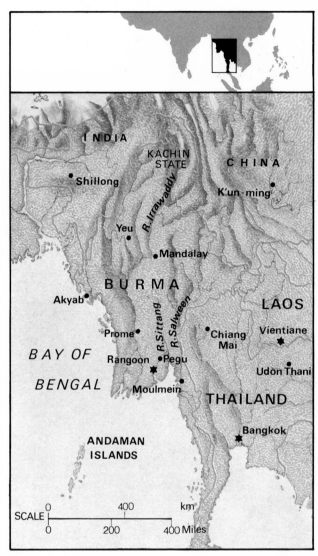

The Buddhist Burmese call their land the Golden Land. It is a fertile country with a population of some 30 million people, bounded by mountains and sea and drained by three mighty rivers, the Irrawaddy, the Sittang and the Salween. It is a land of pagodas, their white and gilded spires piercing the tropical greenery, rising skyward from the tops of hills and mountains. In the fields rice grows green until it ripens when it turns yellow and tawny. Fish proliferate in the canals, streams, rivers and up country lakes where fishermen, standing on one leg, propel their craft with a deft twist of the other, wrapped around an oar. By and large, the Burmese are a religious people. Earnest, ideological powers providing financial aid to buy agricultural machinery have been astonished to find their largesse spent on an extra layer of beaten gold for a Burmese pagoda roof.

In the hilly areas and mountains live the hill tribes, the minority peoples whose culture and way of life is in sharp

In the background of the central market of Mandalay is a *zeygyo* or clock tower designed — surprisingly — by an Italian architect.

The owl behind this woman selling spices is there to ward off evil spirits. Spirit beliefs are older than Buddhist beliefs; both exist together.

contrast to that of the lowland Burmese who make up about 70 per cent of the country's population. There is a vast difference in their physical environments. The hill tribes live in rough mountain terrain where communications are difficult, while the Burmese in the valleys and lowlands lead a far more highly organized economic and political life.

Burma is an ancient land to which, through the centuries, contacts with India, Ceylon and China, and more recently with the Portuguese, French and the British, have brought influences and ideas. These have been adapted to the Burmese mold. From India and Ceylon came Theravada Buddhism, an organized philosophical religion and cosmology, a theory of statecraft, and architecture and art. From China came technology. Even after colonization by the British, which ended in 1948, the new social rules and more rational, impersonal rule of law did not alter the distinctive Burmese character. Their dress, manners and religion were all preserved.

The ordinary Burmese villager lives with his wife and children in a house raised from the ground. Made of bamboo with a palm leaf thatched roof, it is set in its own compound. His wife may even be his first cousin. Some young Burmese couples believe destiny has brought them together to become man and wife in the village. Some say 'put two pots together and they'll crack', and 'put two pieces of rope together and they'll entangle'. Other young people may look for more precise qualities in a partner. The five important qualities of a man are that he is of 'pure race' — meaning that he is free from diseases like leprosy and TB and not a grave-digger or a descendant of a pagoda slave — and that he is educated, rich, and free of the vices of drinking and gambling. The important qualities of a woman are that she is virtuous, a good housewife and cook, attractive and educated.

From the time they are born astrology plays an important part in the life of all Burmese·people. A child's name is chosen according to the day on which he is born, for certain letters of the alphabet are appropriate for 10

(Above) The bustle of a morning vegetable market in Mandalay, the Royal Golden City of Kipling's poetry, also called the Cluster of Gems.

A policeman in Rangoon peacefully enjoys a cheroot. The tattooing on his arms — rarely seen today — is to protect him from evil spirits.

People of Burma

Oxen pull a truck piled high
with teak that has been floated
down the Irrawaddy river:
timber is a major source of
income for Burma.

Villagers draw round a steamer being loaded. The rivers and their tributaries form a system of communication, as well as dictating the Burmese way of life.

(Middle) Valuable timber floats down the Irrawaddy, which meanders slowly through Burma, nourishing the rice fields and providing abundant fish.

certain days. To know the exact time of birth is vital in order to draw up his horoscope. This is inscribed on a piece of bamboo and kept with those of the other members of the family. It is referred to at any time when an astrologer is consulted. Palmistry and astrology are usually combined for the making of predictions.

When a girl and a young man get married both their parents give presents, although it is the man's parents who must pay for the wedding feast if there is one. But frequently a young couple marry in a very simple ceremony. Dressed in their best clothes they sit in an auspicious part of the house, in the east or south, before the village elders, their parents and friends, and one representative from each household in the village. A line of young girls, dressed as the royal maidens once used to dress, stands at the door giving cigars and eugenia leaves for good luck and happiness to the arriving guests. The young couple kneel and bow down till their foreheads almost touch the ground. This they do three times, once for the Buddha, once for his teaching and once for the order of the monks. Then they bow to the elders.

A girl does not change her name when she is married. In Burma, except in Buddhism, men and women are of almost equal status. Even if they divorce there is no particular loss of status, because men and women are equally regarded as individuals within the society. Women can inherit equally with men and, if divorced, the assets of the marriage are equally divided between them. All men, however, are believed to have within them *hoon*, a religious essence which places them on a higher spiritual plane. This is a man's male power and it must be safeguarded by women. So a wife sleeps on the left side of her husband, since this essence is believed to lie in his right side, and keeps her head lower than his. Her clothing, especially her *htamein* – a kind of sarong – and her sandals must never be placed over his head.

Inside a village house there is little furniture but bedding, a low table, a few baskets made of plaited palm leaves with fitted lids in which clothes and other personal belongings are kept, a few pots, a bucket and a kerosene lamp. Other odds and ends hang from hooks on the walls or rafters, or stand on the ledge that runs around the inside walls and which the Burmese call a 'mouse ledge'. In the auspicious part of the house, there is a 'Buddha shelf', a shrine with an image or a picture of the Buddha, vases of flowers, candles, tinsel and paper decorations and miniature plates and cups for food and water offerings. Here too there is a coconut for the household spirit – a large coconut with a v-shaped stalk called the 'mouse's tail' which is replaced every four months. Food offerings are also given to this spirit, but less regularly.

Burmese men wear a sarong-like *longyi* and shirt, and women a blouse with their *htamein*. Usually the girls have their ears pierced while in their mid-teens. They wear powder made from sandalwood bark mixed to a paste with water 'to keep the skin tight' and wear their long,

103

Ducks swim on the river near Pegu: the Burmese like to keep flocks of ducks, both for hunting and for domestic purposes.

People of Burma

oiled hair in a knot on the top or side of the head, with the hair hanging down, or entirely in a neat knot on the back of the head. In the past men were tattooed from the waist to the knees, but now this is rare on a man under forty. Some men however may be tattooed with mythical animals or birds. A more common sight, in villages especially, are tattooed bands around the men's ankles or wrists which are said to guard against snakebites. The dots tattooed on the palms of the hands are to deter the power of witches.

During the busy season in the villages, men and women wake before dawn and spend the morning in the fields. After eating and resting, they return to work. More than 85 per cent of the people in Burma live in villages. The rhythm of the seasons, the phases of the moon—for the Burmese have a lunar calendar— and the agricultural cycle in Burma mingle with the traditional celebrations of Buddhist and spirit rituals. The torrential rains of the monsoon fall between May and October in most of the country. Rivers spill over their banks and the plains are flooded. There are three seasons—the rainy season, the cool season and the hot season—and many events fall regularly each year in the rhythm of seasons.

The Water Festival lasts for three or four days and marks the beginning of the Burmese year. It falls in the month of Tagu which is some time in April or May, and, because of the lunar calendar, not always on the same date. This is not a Buddhist festival, although many people do go to the monasteries to pay their respects to the monks. This is the time when young people pay respect to old people, offering them cool water and sprinkling them with scented water. And it is a time when villagers wash their hair, change their clothes, sweep out the house to wash away the past year's dirt. Thus they begin the new year afresh. Bunches of leaves and twigs are hung by the front door and special pots, filled with water, are placed on a stand outside. For young people this is a gay time. They often completely drench each other with water. It is an opportunity to meet informally, and a young man will find the courage to visit the house of a girl he admires to ask her father if he might sprinkle her with water. It is nearing the end of the dry season and the earth is parched and water supplies are low. Perhaps by throwing water about so extravagantly the Burmese are showing how much faith they have in the imminent arrival of the monsoon.

The full moon of Kahson is Buddha's Day, the day on which the important events in the Buddha's life are commemorated. The base of the banyan tree, the bo tree under which the Buddha reached enlightenment, is watered and in the villages the whole community feeds the monks. This is called *Hsungywek*. By contributing to this special meal for the Buddhist monks the villagers earn merit and in turn improve their karma. Karma is the result of all the good and bad deeds performed in this life and all former lives. The state of a man's karma

(Top) A sign in Mandalay market reads 'Be kind to animals by not eating them' — a plea of the Buddha in the middle of meat selling stalls.

A smiling girl in a bright *htamein* gives Burmese soldiers garlands of jasmine as they parade in Rangoon on an armed forces parade day.

decides the nature of his future incarnations. Feeding the monks in this special way is one of the most important ways of earning merit, although even more important are building a pagoda or a monastery, or giving a well or bell to a monastery.

The Buddhist Lent, Wa, is the three-month period falling at the same time as the rainy season, a time of special religious importance. For the villagers there are many small but important agricultural tasks to be done. The monks are restricted to the monasteries. Travel between villages is difficult during the monsoon and there are no marriage ceremonies, no festivities of any sort and no ordinations of novices or monks. At the end of Lent falls the Festival of Lights which marks Buddha's ascension into the spirit world. Paper candle-lanterns are released into the air 'to light the Buddha's way'.

Then, at the end of October, comes the *Kahtein* ceremony which refers to the cotton cloth used for making the robes woven annually by villagers for the monks. This is the time when the monks are presented with the eight requisites of a monk: three robes, a bowl, a straight razor, a needle, a girdle and a water strainer, although the gifts are not strictly limited to these eight. Even money is given, on a money tree. The gifts are often displayed at a cross-roads near the village for about a week before they are actually presented to the monks.

Next on the calendar is the Lighting Festival of Tazaungmon. Candles are lit at the pagodas on a night when the planets are believed to be in line across the heavens. This is an occasion of great excitement, especially for the unmarried girls, for during the night they weave the 'early robe'. In the villages every household that possibly can sends an unmarried girl to take part. In Rangoon, the capital, teams of girls chosen from each quarter compete. First of all there is a mock planting, plucking, ginning and spinning of the cotton. Then, for the whole night, the girls weave, watched by a large crowd. They are kept awake by eating pickled tea-leaves and by the music of the orchestra.

Between these events are the celebrations and rituals relating to certain stages in people's lives: the naming of a baby, the ordination of a novice or of a monk, the ear-boring ceremony and marriages and funeral rituals which are different for monks and laymen, depending on whether death is natural or 'green' and violent. Only two of these occasions are Buddhist affairs, the others are purely secular. The special meal which is fed to the monks might be given to coincide with the occasion of a marriage or ear-boring ceremony and is always held seven days after, and on the anniversary of, a death.

The ordination of novices is probably the most important religious celebration in Burma. A man is not regarded as being fully Buddhist Burmese, indeed fully a man, unless he has been a novice. A boy may even go through the ceremony more than once so that a relative with no son might be given the opportunity of earning

In a blaze of fire the body
of a dead man is cremated
in his ornate coffin according
to the ceremonies of a
traditional funeral.

the merit which the ceremony gives the sponsor. But for most people it is a once-in-a-lifetime occurrence and so is held when parents can afford the very best display possible. Boys become novices some time between the ages of eight and fifteen. In theory the boy could simply be taken to the monastery and, after having his head shaved, don the yellow robe which all monks and novices wear. But in practice this is an occasion to re-enact the Buddha's own story. The boy is dressed in the finery of a prince resembling Prince Siddhattha who became the last Buddha and rode off on his horse, leaving his life at the palace and his sleeping wife and child. The boy leaves the life of a layman for the life of the monastery. The ear-boring ceremony for young girls often takes place at the same time, when sisters, relatives or friends may have

their ears pierced as part of the celebration.

Brothers, or any group of boys, may become novices together. Before the ceremony takes place the village spirit must be propitiated and the boys go to the village spirit shrine on the first day to make sure that the spirit is appeased and so will not disrupt things. A pavilion is erected, built of cardboard and wood, covered in gilt and paste and glass jewels to imitate Prince Siddhattha's palace. Here the band plays day and night, dancers perform and clowns indulge in amusing the crowd.

On the second day, a special meal is given to the monks in the 'palace'. Following that all the guests eat. Then there is more entertainment. The brocades and gilt ornaments and jewelry and royal costumes worn by the boys and girls, the flowers and gay dress of the guests, the

At the important Shinpiu
ceremony boys re-enact
the life of the Buddha.
Such a ceremony earns the
sponsor much spiritual merit.

(Bottom) Boys being ordained
at a Shinpiu ride in splendor
to the temple, where for a
time they will renounce
the world for the spirit.

A newly widowed Burmese
woman follows her husband's
funeral procession. Although
bereaved she loses no status
for men and women are equal.

delicious foods, the imitation palace, the clowns, dancers
and band all add to the excitement. Sometimes the little
novices-to-be and the girls who will have their ears
pierced, sitting on the raised daïs watching it all, are
completely overwhelmed by the occasion.

After the entertainment the boys ride in a great
procession through the village or neighborhood to the
monastery. Gifts are taken for the monks and also the
things which the young novices will need there. The boys
may ride on ponies, on an elephant, or even in cars. In
the procession young girls are dressed in their prettiest
clothes as royal maidens and carry betel-boxes and 107

The Shwe Dagon Pagoda in Rangoon — the largest Buddhist shrine in Asia and 2,500 years old — is covered in gold leaf, the tip encrusted with jewels.

flowers. Women carry trays of gifts. Boys carry golden umbrellas. The band, clowns and dancing girls are followed by all the friends and relatives.

On returning to the 'palace' the actual ceremony begins. It is conducted by a Master of Ceremonies who has been especially hired for the occasion. He entertains with a mixture of sermons, religious chants, songs, homilies, legends, conversations with the instruments of the band and vulgar jokes. Then the presence of the Buddha is invoked by the band playing a special tune. The novices-to-be are fed with balls of rice, a cotton thread is placed around their necks to protect them from the jealousy of evil spirits, water is sprinkled on their heads and eugenia leaves are placed in their hair. Then all the spirits are invited and offered food. Contributions are collected from the guests and everyone leaves the 'palace'. The boys, in the presence of their parents and the monks, have their heads shaved and they put on the yellow robes before returning to the 'palace' where the concluding ceremony of a sermon and the pouring of water is conducted by monks. The parents announce their merit and share it with the others.

On the third morning the monks are fed again. In the presence of the boys, the parents and a few old people, they pour water and give another short sermon. From then on the novices' connections with the secular world have been severed. They spend their days at the monastery, only leaving it in the morning to go with the other monks on their alms round, when they will probably be given food by their parents, although they must not show by their behavior that there is any special relationship between them. The young novices stay for weeks, months or even years in the monastery — indeed this will probably only be the first of several periods they will spend in the monastery during their lives.

Theravada Buddhism is said to be much stronger in Burma than in any of the other Theravada Buddhist countries. It has become highly interwoven with the folk religion of spirit worship. Spirits, which are called *nats,* are quite different from witches, ghosts and demons. They are supernatural beings who are more powerful than man and who can affect him either for good or evil. There are three main types of spirits of which the most important are the 'thirty-seven *nats*'. The others are the nature *nats* and the *devas*. The 'thirty-seven *nats*' and the nature *nats* may at best be described as neutral, and at worst as evil. The *devas*, who belong to Buddhism, are benevolent and moral. The others are amoral. *Nats* have jurisdiction over cultivated fields, forests and hills. Every house is guarded by a spirit, Lord of the Great Mountain.

What is different about life in the towns and the capital is the absence of the agricultural cycle. Many people work in office jobs with an office routine. They tell the time by the clock not by descriptive phrases, as do the villagers for whom the sun and daily physical events mark the

time. Villagers note the time in the morning as 'when the

Worshippers bringing offerings
rest in the cool of the Kuang
Hmu Daw Pagoda at Sagaiang,
not far from Mandalay
in northern Burma.

Just as Buddha shaved off his
hair and eyebrows to symbolize
his renunciation of worldly
things, so must young boys
at Shinpiu – ordination.

sun is as high as a toddy palm' (7 to 8 am), and 'the time
when monks return from their begging round' (9 to
10 am). In the evening there is 'the time when even ugly
people look beautiful' (twilight), 'the time when two
brothers can't recognise each other' (6 to 7 pm) and 'the
time when the young bachelors return home' (10 to 11
pm). In the towns there is more organized entertainment.
Films are popular and there are bigger markets. There
are hospitals, schools and universities. But between the
Buddhist Burmese agriculturalists' way of life and that of
the hill peoples there is still a very great difference.

Burma's political borders with Bangla Desh, India,
China, Laos and Thailand create unnatural divisions
between peoples of the same or related ethnic groups.
The majority of the Naga live in India and similarly, the
Chin, Kachin, Shan, Karen and Mong belong to groups
who live on both sides of Burma's political boundaries.
The Shan for example, who make up about 7 per cent of
Burma's population, are Tai-speaking Buddhist people
of which there are about 30 million spread over South-
east Asia – more than the total population of Burma.
Frontiers of language do not necessarily correspond with
frontiers of culture and political power.

There are many obvious differences between hill and
valley or lowland peoples. The hill people live in rough,
mountainous terrain where they practise shifting cultivation, while the valley people live where they can grow
wet rice, in the lowlands and valleys. Although racially
the same, hill and valley peoples have distinctly different
ways of life. Because wet rice cultivation supports a large
number of people living together in one locality, there is
greater cultural unity within valley groups. The Shan, for
instance, who are valley people living in the Shan State in
the north-east of Burma, usually live in villages of
between 200 and 500 people. Their bamboo houses are
built on piles about eight feet above the ground, with a
ladder leading up to a veranda. As well as irrigated rice,
they grow tobacco, cotton, sugar cane and maize, and
breed horses, water buffalo, pigs and chickens. There are

109

At the same Shinpiu ceremony
new initiates squat in their
saffron colored monks' robes
and begin the meditations and
prayers of their new life.

Like the evocative old stations of the British Raj in India, this sleepy Burmese station with an old steam train and crowded platform is English too.

(Bottom) People who cannot read or write can always hire the services of typewriter scribes at any street corner to compose their letters.

two main classes in Shan society, nobility and commoners. Although most Shan, of course, are commoners and although today the Shan princes have lost most of the autonomy they once had, they still enjoy the loyalty of the majority of Shan.

The shifting-cultivation hill people, by contrast, practise a type of farming which supports far fewer people and so their settlements are small and widely scattered. The Kachin, who are hill people living in the mountain areas in the north and north-east of Burma, live in villages on mountain ridges. Most households are self-sufficient. Their basic crop is rice, grown by slash-and-burn farming on the forested hillsides, but they also grow maize, sesame, millet and tobacco. There is a very important difference between the type of leadership of hill and valley peoples. Through the centuries India has had a great influence on the valley people in politics and religion. But China has influenced the hill peoples in a quite different way, mainly through trade. The hill chieftain's position is traditionally inherited, or sometimes achieved by giving a series of sacrificial feasts, as do the southern Chin, the hill people who live in the west of Burma. By contrast a valley prince is a charismatic figure,

Elephants in the teak forests haul heavy logs through the undergrowth. Money is spent on pagodas and offerings rather than on machinery.

The Burmese year begins with the Water Festival, when everyone drenches each other with water, 'the liquid seed', symbol all over the world of the life force.

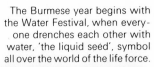

with great individual authority. While a hill chieftain might give women in marriage to other groups as a pledge of economic co-operation the prince in the valley receives women as tribute; he never gives women away to outsiders.

The hill peoples speak a great variety of languages. Burmese, the language of the lowland majority, has never been their mother tongue. But it is common to find hill people who are bilingual, speaking Burmese or Shan as well as their own language. The languages of the valley peoples, although diverse, are far fewer. The main religion of the hill people is animism and usually involves some kind of ancestor worship. In the main room of a Kachin house there is a special area which is sacred to the household spirits as well as to any ancestral spirits which have not yet gone to the land of the dead. In front of the house there are altars to the spirits. The valley people, on the other hand, are Buddhist. Occasionally hill peoples become Buddhists and are assimilated into the way of life of the valley people. Sometimes whole groups have become economically sophisticated and have adopted the religion and the manners of their neighbors in the valley, as some Palaung have done. The Shan have gradually assimilated many neighboring peoples over the centuries, with little effect on their own culture. Various Kachin groups have adopted Buddhism and the Shan language and political structure, and have in effect become Shan. Because of this it is possible for a person to start life as a member of one group and end up as a member of quite a different group. Hill peoples, however, tend usually to have much more in common with other hill peoples – even with those who live great distances away from them – than they have with their nearer neighbors in the valleys. Hill and valley peoples usually remain separate except for their dependence on each other's products. The hill peoples exchange their forest products like special types of wood, bamboo and beeswax with their valley neighbors for glaze for beer pots, brass pots and other sophisticated metals.

Moken
Burma

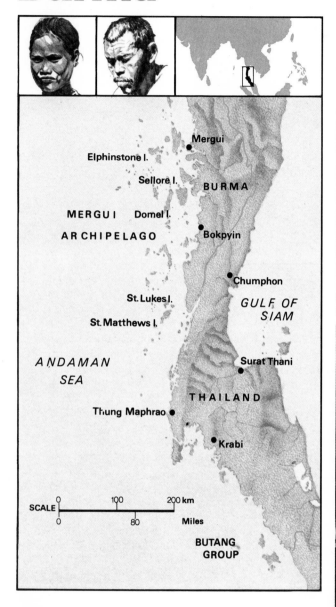

The Moken are a nomadic, sea-going people who live largely on boats in the Mergui archipelago off the Burmese coast. In and around this north-south chain of over two hundred islands, lying between the Burmese coast and the Andaman islands across the sea, the Moken are so elusive that no one can currently tell how many of them there are. At the last count, in 1943, there were an estimated 4,000 families of Moken.

Early in the 19th century there were, however, far fewer. In 1828 it was reported that 'a race of men called *Chalon* and *Pase* by the Burmese have spread through the Mergui archipelago. Their fear of the Malays and other pirates has obliged these poor creatures to adopt a very unstable mode of life. During the north-east monsoon

113

The Moken seem oblivious of
the fishy débris that litters
the boats they live on: to
throw this garbage overboard
would be to invite the sharks.

they have to flee to the more isolated islands to avoid being taken as slaves by the Malays, Siamese or Burmese. These men seem to be peaceful and industrious. The whole tribe consists at most of 400 people.'

The Moken's way of life, apparently, was not unstable. Rather, their ways were lasting and their numbers had increased. But in more recent years this stability might, curiously, be attributed to the addiction of so many Moken to opium. Opium traders and pedlars have a strong hold over the Moken and this permits few to change their way of life. They must trade their shell-fish and oysters, snails and sea-worms for other necessities of life like rice, salt and clothing. And the same traders, whether Malay or Chinese, also the men who supply the Moken with opium.

Today the Burmese call the Moken the Selon, Selong or Selung. But in the Moken's own language, their name is derived from *oken* (salt water) and *lemo* (to dip) and roughly translated means 'immersed in the sea'. Although there are related groups who once led a similar sea-gypsy life in other parts of South-east Asia along the west coast of Malaya and throughout much of Indonesia, many of these people have returned to the shore-based life and become assimilated with the land-bound people around them. Only the Moken remain 'immersed in the sea' in the old style – although admittedly this has been on a diminishing scale since World War II.

The Moken are small people with a fairly high fore-head, wavy but not curly hair, and dark brown skin. They are gracefully built and muscular, and the women in particular have a distinctive beauty. Individuals vary widely in type and appearance. Many display clear signs of Chinese, Malay or Negrito ancestry. Both sexes wear the sarong although the men sometimes replace this with a loin-cloth. All go naked above the waist. They speak a number of different Malayo-Polynesian dialects, which vary so widely that it is often hard for a Malay speaker to understand a Moken. Indeed a Moken will not always find it easy to converse with another Moken from a different group.

They came, apparently, from somewhere in the region of the Malacca Straits. Their own oral tradition refers to their mainland origin, and to incessant harassment and exploitation by the Malays which drove them northwards and eventually – in desperation – to take refuge in a water-based, semi-fugitive existence. They seem to have the history, and they certainly have the psychology, of a refugee people. They are suspicious of strangers, and several travelers have reported that their suspicions seem to deepen rather than to ease as the time of a visitor's stay goes on.

After fruitless attempts by the Burmese authorities to control and tax them the Moken proved ungovernable and were finally dismissed, ignored and left to go their own way, much as land gypsies are dismissed in some countries.

The flesh of sea snails is boiled and sold to the Chinese as a delicacy; the empty shells provide valuable mother-of-pearl.

When on shore, the men are
busy repairing the boats.
The women dig in the sand
and collect worms which
they consider delicious.

The Moken are slightly built
with wavy hair and dark
brown skin. Both men and
women wear the sarong and
all go naked above the waist.

Sea slugs' and sea snails'
flesh has to be boiled for
20 minutes and then dried
over slow fires before
it can be sold.

The long pole with which this
woman propels her boat
becomes a dangerous harpoon
for catching large fish when
a barbed tip is added.

The Moken live up to their aquatic name. They are expert swimmers, divers and, above all, seamen. Their boats are ideal for their purpose. Light and stable, roomy enough to carry eight or nine people, they can stand up to the worst storms of the Andaman Sea. Their boats and huts are strewn with garbage, swarming with vermin, and suffused with the stench of rotting fish. Even at sea they never throw fish-entrails and other food-waste overboard, but allow it to accumulate in the bottom of the boat. This has the advantage of not leaving a trail of waste which would tempt sharks to follow the Moken boats around.

Each boat belongs to an individual man, and is built by collective effort from the trunk of a *hopea odorata,* a tree which abounds in the islands. The tree trunk is hollowed out and widened by a process of heating and stretching to form a kind of low canoe. (The Moken acquire their axes and adzes for this by trade.) The curved sides are constructed from long strips cut from the *vingan* palm which, after they are gathered and stripped of their outer bark, provide a light, porous, absorbent material, which swells on contact with water. The result is a completely watertight boat that needs no caulking and no nails, for the boat is held together by wood and bamboo pegs and strands of rattan and pliable creepers. An open slatted bamboo deck, a mast, and an earthen fireplace complete the structure. At one end there is often a rough hut of sticks, roofed with palm-leaves, but this is detachable and

116

As springs are rare in the
archipelago, water must be
stored on the boat. This
woman is carrying water in
a section of bamboo.

is often taken ashore and used as a hut on dry land.

The Moken propel their boats expertly, by poles, oars and rectangular sails, made from screw-palm or pandanus leaves, softened by heat, straightened out by rolling, and then sewn together with rattan threads. The boats are not permanent structures. They rot steadily from the start and only last for two years at the most. For as long as they last they stand in need of constant repair. At every stopping-place, therefore, while the women gather food, the men replenish the stock of stripped *vingan* wood which serves as their repair-kit. When the Moken are not actually at sea they are largely occupied in boat-building.

It is not only the search for food which keeps the restless Moken constantly on the move. So does their overwhelming anxiety to avoid all contact with strangers. The Moken stay together in the *kabang* or mobile floating village, the fleet of ten to forty boats, each one the permanent home of a single family. The people of each *kabang* keep very much to themselves. If two groups happen to land their boats in the same bay, they settle at opposite ends of it and keep apart. When on land they usually live either in the huts which they temporarily detach from their boats, or else in the boats themselves which they beach for security and maintenance. The Moken have neither chiefs nor any kind of formally constituted leadership. There is only an informal leadership exercised by the oldest men and the most skilful fishermen and navigators.

But the Moken do have people akin to priests. Their most important religious belief is in a number of spirits, some good, some evil, who command all natural forces and all disasters. All of these spirits demand propitiation partly by means of carved and painted wooden posts, which are erected on some islands in the spirits' honor, and partly by sacrifices of roots, shells, rice, chickens, opium and blood, to enlist the help and protection of the kinder spirits. The offering is made by a shaman (*micha blen*) on behalf of the group. The gifts are placed in square sacrificial bowls, a candle is lit and the shaman enters into a state of trance or possession and so communicates with the spirits.

The shaman is a healer as much as a 'priest' in the religious sense, and having sent his patients also into a state of trance or possession, he works on them, trembling and quivering with the impact of his encounter with the unseen. His task may be to undo the work of his evil counterpart the witch (*micha bap*), who is a dangerous man, since he can cause sickness or death by manipulating a wax image of his victim or a little sand from one of his footprints. But it is believed that most illnesses are caused by evil spirits, some of which are equated with the souls of dead people, to whom any wound or injury gives access into the body. If it is they who are the cause of the sickness, it is the shaman's task to suck them forth – having first gone into his trance and invoked supernatural powers – and then spit them out into the wind. If the patient recovers, he will often change his name so as to confuse the spirits and discourage them from returning to the attack.

The Moken traditionally dispose of their dead by exposure. They build a low platform on a special deserted cemetery, place the dead man upon it and leave him there. Alternatively they put his body in his boat, which they cut in two, so that one half can hold the body while the other acts as a lid – a suitable mausoleum for a man whose whole life has been centered around his boat.

Moken boats provide no privacy and the intimate circumstances of marriage, birth and death tend to be public events. Moken generally marry members of their own *kabang*. The marriage is initially agreed by the couple concerned, and then formally negotiated by an embassy of 'joiners' sent on the man's behalf to the boat of the girl's parents. Occasionally, however, a young man will make a prolonged visit to another *kabang*. He will live and work there and finally marry a girl there. Until the first child is born a married couple normally lives with the man's parents. Then the father sets up his own household. This means building his own boat with the help of relations and friends, where he may establish his family. On each family boat live an average of seven people.

The Moken have a very simple technology. Boats and sleeping mats are their basic requirements. Grasses, lianas and bast-fiber provide them with good cordage, and the women make clay pots as required. They carve and paint tall poles and erect them to propitiate the spirits. And they manifest a creativity in the stories which they tell, sagas and folk-tales which, though not wholly their own, display a marked degree of imagination and wit in the telling.

But their overwhelming occupation is in simply maintaining their subsistence economy, by land and sea. Although the seas are lavish their catches, secured by nothing more effective than a spear, are small. Despite their heavy dependence on the sea, and the technical inventiveness displayed in their boat-building, they have never worked out for themselves the possibilities of nets and fish-hooks. Where these tools are used at all, they are an innovation from outside. When the boats come to anchor by a beach the women go ashore and look for food. A special delicacy is the sand-worm, *phymosoma japonicum*, which the women find by plugging the entrance to the large hole in which it lives and then digging it out with sticks.

When the tide goes out they gather shellfish from the beach: mostly oysters and limpets, with an occasional giant clam. They eat these when they gather them, according to the vagaries of the tide. As soon as any single beach has been fully harvested there is a need to move on in search of fresh pastures. And it is this that keeps the Moken constantly on the move, making them into real nomads or gypsies. The sight of a giant ray, for

117

Moken Burma

After a hard day's fishing
men gather to smoke opium.
The drug is mixed with banana
leaves and inhaled through a
bamboo water pipe.

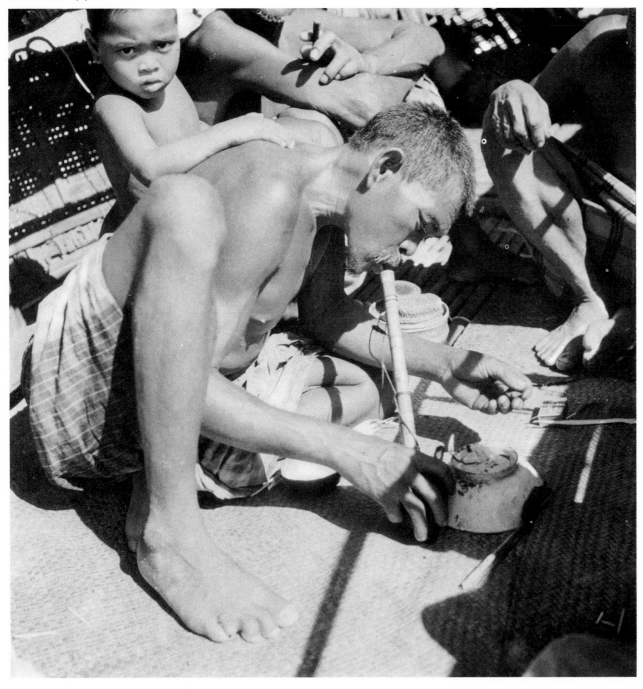

example, which offers the prospect of a deeply-relished variation upon the normal diet, will send them, after much excitement and preparation, off in pursuit of it. The huge fish is speared, dragged ashore and then cut into long narrow strips which will be dried in the sun to preserve it.

The Moken also hunt with trained dogs for wild pigs and deer. And they gather fruit, berries, roots, and honey. Although by long tradition they are a self-sufficient people, they have in recent generations come to have needs which they cannot meet without trade; for rice in particular, but also for salted fish, knives and axes and other iron implements, pots and pans, goggles for pearl-diving, and – outstandingly – opium. They are well placed for trading for they have readily to hand three commodities which are in sufficient demand elsewhere to enable them to escape from the limitations of their subsistence economy. There is the sea-slug or holothurian, which they spear in quantities in fairly deep water, boil in cauldrons, dry over slow fires, and then sell as a delicacy to the Chinese market. Then there is the *siput* or sea-snail, which they prepare the same way as the sea-slug, and sell to the same market. Its shell has a further great value for mother-of-pearl – a form of wealth for which the Moken have at times been envied, harried and killed. Then, finally, there is the pearl-oyster, which they gather with no technical aids beyond a pair of goggles. They dive for the pearl-oysters in teams, each team sharing the reward of its success. Their efforts are repaid in the highly-esteemed currency of opium.

With these three principal commodities to offer, and with amber, tanbark, cordwood, edible birds' nests and a rich ore of tin on one island, the Moken are indeed well placed for trading. The great obstacle is their timidity. But within limits this can be overcome; and while the Moken retain their deep suspicion of the outside world in general, they can be made to trust the individual trader, Chinese or Malay, who comes to deal with them.

The Chinese trader typically associates with a Moken group, lives with it, marries into it, conducts his bartering on a day-to-day basis to his own profit, and protects and defends the group as necessary. A Malay trader will operate on a different basis, dealing with three or four *kabangs* at once and meeting them from time to time by appointment to barter with them. This trade benefits the Moken, for it provides them with useful commodities which they would otherwise be deprived of. But it also has a drawback, for they become dependent upon the trader, partly for food and safety, but above all for opium. Carefully, in a controlled way, the trader has turned them into addicts over the years, so that they will do almost anything for him rather than endanger their supply of the precious drug. They are thus under his control, and will continue to sell their produce at a fraction of its market worth. And on the other side, as though by agreement, these traders refrain from bidding

The Moken hack the hull from a tree trunk, and add long strips of *vingan* palm—which swell when saturated – to form watertight curved sides.

(Bottom) When a Moken becomes a father his fellow *kabang* members will help him build his own boat and set up his own household and family

against each other and from acting in any way that might affect the terms of trade in the Moken's favor. They also do all they can to retain this closed market by carefully fostering the Moken's inborn fear of all officials and strange men and boats.

The Moken have no illusions about the men who thus exploit them. Their word for a trader is *nyuko*, 'a very bad man'. But the choice, as they see it, is between being exploited by one man and being at the mercy of all the world; and they choose the lesser evil. Thus they gain a kind of security and stability, but at the cost of economic, if not physical, captivity and at the greater cost of more or less permanent and universal opium-addiction.

Padaung
Burma

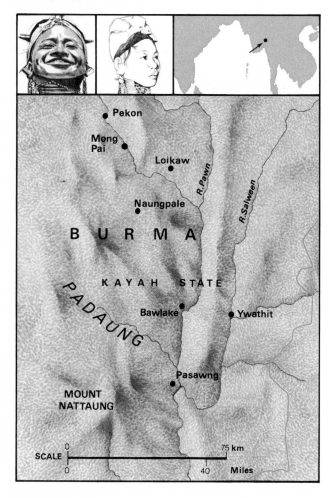

the neck unable to support the head without assistance. If the rings are removed, the head simply lolls uncontrollably to one side. This situation is exploited in order to safeguard the women's virtue. The penalty for infidelity is to have them removed so that the unfortunate adulteress has to spend the rest of her life lying down or else holding her head in her hands.

Neck rings are worn principally for decoration and beauty, to indicate wealth and position and to enhance the wearer's value in the marriage system. The Padaung claim that they were first worn as a protection against tiger bites, tigers being common in the parts of China from where they originally came. Tigers certainly attack the throat.

In fact what each Padaung woman wears are not rings at all but a long spiral, once of gold but now usually of copper, which is coiled into position and then often ornamented in various ways by attaching coins, bangles, and other bright objects to it. The immediate problem it creates is how to wash the neck. Cleanliness is necessary since sweat would otherwise cause verdigris to collect on the rings leading to sores on the neck. Padaung women solve this problem by sliding a damp cloth between the neck and the rings, pulling it smartly up and down so that it cleans the neck and polishes the rings at the same time. They do this twice a day.

Little Padaung girls, if they are to follow the custom of wearing rings, start at about five years old. They look forward to the first occasion and prepare for it for some time in advance by pulling at each other's heads and stretching each other's necks. Fitting the first rings is accompanied by a ceremony. The village medicine-man, the *bedin-saya,* chooses the date carefully after consulting the omens. The village is decorated, and a lot of rice wine is drunk. For a whole day the little girl's neck is massaged and rubbed with a secretly formulated ointment that is supposed to soften her skin. Then, for an hour, her head is twisted and pulled. Finally while the girl's mother stands behind her and pulls her chin upwards and back, the *bedin-saya* works the first, four-inch, spiral into place. To ease the initial pain, the spiral is separated from the jaw and collar-bone by cloth pads. But in her pride in this new womanly adornment, a girl will usually remove the pads as soon as she can bear to.

Two years later a second and deeper spiral will be fitted. Already the girl's neck will have ceased to support her head, so that her mother will have to carry its weight carefully after the old spiral comes off and until the new one is safely in place. Progressively over the years new rings are fitted until the head looks tiny and detached, precariously balanced on top of a high copper column. At the peak of her glory a Padaung woman will not be able to see her baby while suckling it. She will not be able to see her own feet or the ground around her without bending from the waist. And furthermore she will probably wear similar spirals around her legs.

The word Padaung means 'long neck' and is the name given to a small group of people in Burma who, like certain African peoples, elongate their necks to three or four times their natural length by wearing a number of gold or copper rings. This practice is far from common in Burma. It is done only by the Padaung women.

The Padaung are part of a larger group known as the Karen (pages 126-129). They live about six hundred miles north-north-east of Rangoon in the state of Kayah on the Thailand frontier. Until recently, to within living memory, the men were warlike headhunters and their society was matrilineal. Then, after a number of murderous wars had killed a high proportion of males and given a certain scarcity value to the survivors, polygamy set in and with it greater male authority. But even now a Padaung will speak of the village women as being a law unto themselves and beyond the reach of any male authority.

Today the habit of wearing neck rings is in a sense dying out and is coming to be regarded as rather old-fashioned. An increasing number of Padaung girls are refusing to wear them. But their elders cannot abandon them for even in early childhood wearing rings soon makes

120

Instituted as a sign of female elegance, this spiral coil ensures fidelity. When, as a punishment, it is removed, the neck breaks.

Lua
Thailand

A Lua woman brews rice liquor,
which Lua men say helps them
get going in the morning and
relaxes them at night. It is
also drunk as a medicine.

As Lua boys and girls grow up they visit each other in groups late at night, and sit and talk or sing songs. If two of them fall in love they leave the group and meet each other alone. The boy gives his girl presents – silver pipes, tobacco and matches. If she accepts them she shows that she is willing to marry him. Both discuss the matter with their parents, but no date is set for the marriage. The girl knows only that she is getting married, not when.

One night when all the village is sleeping, the boy, with some friends, steals to the girl's house. They rush in and drag her screaming away with them. Her father runs to the village elders, wakes them up and tells them that his daughter has been abducted. The elders then go to the groom's house. Here the groom's father tells the elders that the couple want to get married. All the relatives of both families are then brought together to discuss the bride-price. This is done with much drinking, joking and haggling – although the bride-price is in fact fixed traditionally at 16 old silver pieces. Once the haggling is over the groom's and bride's families hold a seven-day series

123

When the rice harvest is over the Lua turn to building and repairing their houses. Here a roof is re-thatched with dried grass.

of feasts attended by all the village. The most important part of the wedding ceremonies is the introduction of the spirits of the bride's ancestors to those of the groom, for the Lua believe that in all things the spirits must be consulted and appeased.

The Lua are the descendants of the original inhabitants and rulers of Thailand and live deep in the hills of northern Thailand near Burma. They say they retreated to these mountains about 900 years ago when their king, Khun Luang Wilanka, was defeated in a magical contest with Cham Tewi, queen of the Mon people. The king wanted to marry the queen, but she said that first he must throw a spear to her palace, a distance of about 25 miles. His first throw fell short, and the queen told him to try again, but before he did so, she tied a piece of magic cloth from her skirt around his head; this weakened him so that he could hardly lift the spear and he and his followers had to flee, to where today about 10,000 Lua live in scattered villages in the mountains where they pursue their traditional way of life in peace. Many other Lua, however, living closer to the plains and valleys have become assimilated into Thai ways of life, and have even become Buddhist.

In the Lua mountain village, life centers around rice. Every year in February the village head – the semang – goes out with the elders to select the fields, which are always a few hours walk away from the village, for planting. The Lua are slash and burn farmers who use a field for one year and then leave it fallow for the next seven to ten years. The selection of rice fields is anything but random. They do not, for example cut down virgin forest which they believe to be the home of powerful spirits. They also leave the area around their village untouched so that it acts as a firebreak, and keeps the village cool and beautiful to look at. When the semang and elders have selected the fields they return with a little of the soil. In the village they sacrifice a chicken and examine its gall bladder. If it is fat, shiny and full of liquid the villagers know they have selected the right fields. If not, another site must be chosen. Once the fields have been allocated – the semang has the first choice – each field-owner must again sacrifice a chicken and examine its gall bladder. If the omen is bad he must exchange his fields with another villager. This continues until he receives a good omen. The Lua believe that to plant in spite of a bad omen will result in a poor rice crop, which if eaten would cause the owner to become ill and die.

Before the rice seeds can be planted the Lua must clear the fields by burning. The date for this is decided by the village elders. Early in the morning on the appointed day the old women of the village invoke the spirits of their ancestors. This occasion, with the end of the harvest, are the only times when Lua women participate in the spirit worship. Along the path to the upland fields the old men place altars for twelve spirits. Sacrifices are made to all 124 but one, for the Lua fear that if all twelve spirits are

After the bride-price is agreed lengths of cotton are wound round the wrists of the bride and groom to ensure peace, long life and happiness.

Apart from rice the Lua grow cotton which a Lua wife must card and clean before it is spun to make clothes for her family.

appeased the fire will burn too well, and they will not be able to control it. Meanwhile in the fields the young men are waiting. At noon if the wind is in the right direction they take a mouthful of rice liquor which they spit on the torches as they are lit. This is to encourage the fire spirits to burn the fields just as the liquor burns their throats. The young men run along the fields touching off a crackling blaze which can be seen and heard for miles.

A few weeks later the semang gives the order for the planting to begin. Before it begins, several chickens, a pig and a dog are sacrificed to the forest spirits and to the spirits of the streams that drain the fields. Then, with a group of friends and relatives, each family starts the planting. Early in the morning the young men move across the field dibbling holes in the ground with long, iron-tipped sticks, each of which has a gong device at the top, which rings every time the stick is poked in the earth. Girls, women and the older men follow, throwing the seeds into the holes. At mid-day everybody stops for lunch. After the meal the young men sing traditional songs, joke with the girls and give them rice liquor to drink. Then everyone returns to work till evening. The planting takes several weeks and when it is finished, about halfway through May, the semang makes yet another sacrifice of a pig (substituted by a buffalo every fifth year) to ensure that the rains will come. Each family contributes to the cost of the animal sacrificed, and receives a portion of the carcass after a little has been offered to the spirits.

During the next few months, as the crops grow, the Lua hold various ceremonies and sacrifices to make sure that they will be successful. During November and December the rice is harvested and taken back to the village to be stored in barns.

The ceremony at the end of the harvest is the most elaborate of all the Lua ceremonies. The village is closed to outsiders and nobody is allowed to leave it. In the morning of the great day each family cooks a chicken, and takes it on a woven mat to two altars erected by the young men. Placed next to the altars, to which a pig is tied, are wooden guns, spears and swords. Small bits of the chicken are taken for sacrificing, and then the families return to their homes where they eat the rest outside the house. The pig is then killed and distributed among the villagers.

After this ceremony, which marks the end of the agricultural year, the Lua turn their attention to marriage and to maintaining their village. This is the time when they build new houses – of woven bamboo walls raised on stilts with steeply pitched roofs covered with thatch – and repair old ones. And at this time of year the Lua worship the house spirits who live in the front walls of their homes. The Lua are careful to build their houses at different angles to each other. One house must be far enough away from the next so that rain falling from one roof on no account mixes with that from the next, for otherwise the occupants will become ill.

125

This Lua woman must stand as still as possible in the rushing torrent of the stream if she is to scoop up the fish lurking under the rocks.

Karen
Thailand

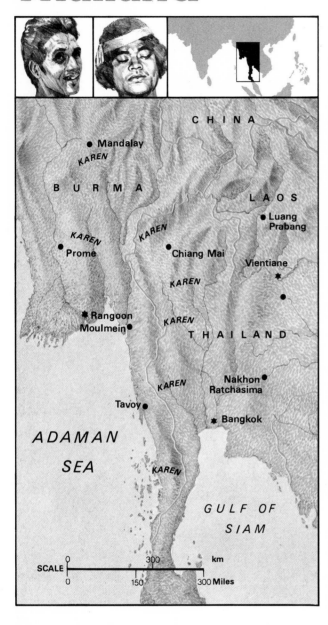

In the hills of the frontier region between Burma and Thailand the Karen build their villages on the steep slopes close by the forest which they will cut and burn during the coming year. Sometimes the villages are surrounded by stockades to keep out marauding animals and in the old days to lend a certain security from the raids of other tribes. The main buildings are long houses and granaries in which they store the rice.

The long houses are built of bamboo and accommodate as many as thirty families in apartments which open onto a central corridor, each with a veranda on the outer side. As well as these family quarters, there is also a *blaw*, a room which serves as both a bachelors' room and

In the highlands Karen farmers
live in the rhythm of the
seasons. The first monsoon
storms signal the time for
planting the rice seedlings.

Burning a field is an anxious time. A good rice crop depends on a good burn. Here a man throws salt on a tray to 'control' the flames.

Karen villagers carry bamboo to build fences and shelters for the new field. In the past whole villages would shift when the men burned new fields.

When rice fails to grow well, the Karen believe it is because the rice spirit strays. Here a man tempts the recaptured spirit with rice liquor.

accommodation for guests. The village is moved frequently, every few years, for in these parts the Karen slash-and-burn farmers quickly exhaust the land.

At the time when a new long house must be built, the village chief will discuss the matter at length with the elders and seek out a new site. It is the hot season, the crops have been harvested and stored and the men can now turn their attention to building. In the past it was always necessary to choose a site that could be easily defended; for there were frequent raids between neighboring villages, chiefly affairs of vengeance. But these were rarely long-lasting feuds and were usually followed by peace-making ceremonies and negotiations by which the losing village was able to regain some of its lost trophies and weapons. And then another important consideration for the village chief before choosing a new site was the will of the spirits. He consulted omens, divining the wishes of spirits with the aid of chicken bones. If these were propitious then the men began the work of cutting bamboo for the new long house. For centuries the Karen, at one and half million strong one of the largest of Southeast Asia's hill tribes, have lived under the authority of other peoples, whether Burmese, Mon, Shan, Thai or British, but under varying degrees of effective control. In some hilly regions of their homeland in south-eastern

Burma and western Thailand the control of their over-lords has always been small. In many other places, and among many of the Karen, the cultural influences of other peoples have been profound – in the Shan states of Burma the Karen have organized themselves on the Shan pattern though with rulers of Karen ancestry. Elsewhere their way of life remains characteristic of the Karen ways which have been followed for centuries. The main feature of this life is the autonomy of the village.

A Karen village in the hills is full of noise. There are many yelping dogs, some of which are trained for hunting, and a host of other noisy animals like pigs and chickens. In the Irrawaddy and Sittang delta regions, Karen either breed horses or skilfully handle elephants which they catch and train themselves. In the hills, however, the slash-and-burn farming, hunting, gathering and fishing takes up most of their time. Karen catch game in nets during group hunts, or they kill it with crossbows or spears. Above all, the staple food of these Karen is rice, boiled and eaten with the other vegetables they grow, or with a curry. Their Burmese neighbors maintain that the Karen will eat anything, be it fish, meat, insect or grain.

In western Thailand, among the Pwo Karen – one of the largest Karen sub-groups – the villagers make all their own clothes. The clothes of Pwo villagers are ornate and bright, woven from cotton grown around the village. The *hse*, a garment like a smock which reaches down to the calves, is characteristic among most of the Karen hill tribes. Single girls habitually wear a long *hse* with red decorations. They also weave shorter red *hses* which they wear with a *ni* or skirt when they are married.

Young men and women meet on occasions like weddings and funerals. But should a boy wish to visit a girl at other times, he must follow certain rules. He must take his harp and appear before her house. He sits down and serenades her, singing to the accompaniment of his instrument. If the girl replies she does so in verse, with a jew's-harp. Then he may climb the ladder to her apartment. If too long an interval elapses without the sounds of their voices singing or their instruments playing, their elders are likely to appear to find out the reason.

Although the hill Karen have never been noted as keen traders, they nevertheless do trade with Burmese or Shan merchants. The cotton cloth, spun, dyed and woven in the Karen villages is exchanged for mats and baskets woven from rattan and bamboo in the Burmese markets. In Thailand it seems that trade is becoming increasingly important in their lives. Here they trade their cotton cloth, forest products, game and meat from their domestic animals, for rice, pottery, salt and fish pastes. The bronze drums they obtain from Shan traders are said to be highly valued among most Karen. These contacts with their neighbors have not passed without other exchanges. The most significant of these is Buddhism. In Burma the vast majority of Karen, whether hill or plain dwellers, are Buddhists. Only the Kayah, south of the Shan state, have been regarded as predominantly animist.

And yet, among many of the hill Karen, the ancient beliefs in supernatural spirits persist. Three distinct religious conceptions seem to have left their mark on the Karen. The principle underlying their ideas is that of an impersonal power which resides in all men and things. It is invisible, and only betrays itself by its effect on certain things. A few individuals, by its aid, are able to perform unusual tasks or even magical deeds; these are persons of *pgho*. The second of their religious conceptions is that every mountain and stream, every season, every object and utensil is possessed of a spirit. Some are benevolent, such as those which watch over births. Others are malevolent and must be appeased with offerings, sacrifices and taboos. And then there is a third religious conception, the tradition of the *Y'wa*, a legend which tells of the placing of the first parents in a garden by the creator.

The village chief leads his villagers in the propitiation of both nature and local spirits, and a senior woman presides over ritual offerings to ancestral spirits. There is also a shaman-sorcerer in the village who will divine the future or the nature of an illness while possessed by a spirit. A medical practitioner employs drugs and magic to treat illnesses. Birth or death are accompanied by many ceremonies which ritually approach the supernatural. Various stages in the agricultural cycle are marked by rites to appease still more spirits. In every aspect of life the spirits, whether offended or merely malicious, may interfere with the Karen. Illness, accident and death are all caused by their activity. Remedies made from plants or herbs may be used to cure the sick, but the only true therapy is through those rites which remove the influence of malevolent spirits or recover an errant soul which has strayed from the body.

129

Even among the highland Karen, the traditional village long houses have sometimes been replaced by single houses where only one family lives.

Shan
Burma

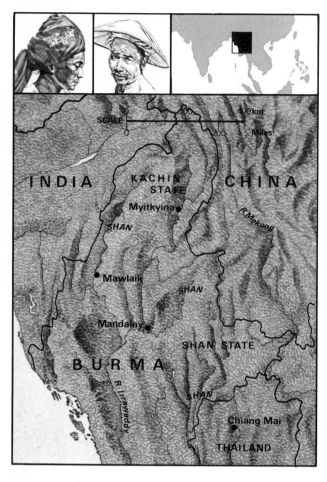

The villages of the Shan people are always built in the valleys and lowlands which run down from the mountains of eastern Burma. The houses are strung out along the river banks, or clustered together in the middle of a group of rice fields. Often groves of bamboo or palms surround the village, and tall grasses grow beside the river. The size of the village depends primarily on the number of rice fields and the extent of the valley lands available for its use. There may be only ten houses, or more than fifty, and larger villages will also include a number of hamlets on the outskirts.

At one end of the village, pagodas, monasteries, shrines and rest-houses – all of which are essential to the religious life of the community – are grouped together. And then at the center is the market place. On certain days this is the focus of all activity; instead of a quiet, sleepy place, the village becomes bustling and a certain excitement fills the air and the voices of the men and women in the street. All other work ceases on these days.

The houses in a Shan village are built almost entirely of bamboo and raised as high as ten feet off the ground to avoid the river floods and as a protection from wild animals. A stout wooden stair or bamboo ladder leads

131

A Shan woman is dressed in
imitation of a legendary bird-
woman. Belief in spirits
co-exists happily with a devout
adherence to Buddhism.

up to the house itself. The floors are of split bamboo; the walls made of woven bamboo mats. The tall river grasses are used to make roof thatches. Only the village headman's house is likely to be larger than 20 feet or so and to be more substantially built with wooden floors and walls. In front of the living compartments of every house there is a veranda partially shaded by a fan shaped roof. Inside, in two or three rooms, the largest of which serves as the living room, kitchen and laundry room, lives the household: a man, his wife and children and possibly a few dependent relatives. In the corner of the living room is a fireplace which, in the winter months, burns throughout the day and night. There is no chimney and smoke escapes through cracks in the walls. The family use the open space beneath the house as a general work area – to pound rice, to dry tobacco and weave mats. Here they store wood and tether buffalo and cattle during the night.

The word Shan is the name the Burmese give to the one and a quarter million Tai people who live in Burma. The people call themselves Tai. As early as the pre-Christian era the Tai entered the region of northern Burma and by the 7th century AD small kingdoms had begun to emerge. In the 13th century the Mongols' defeat of the Burmese Pagan dynasty permitted the Shan to step into the power vacuum. By 1500 most of what is now Burma was a loose federation of domains ruled by Shan princes. The 16th century however also saw the resurgence of Burmese power, which gradually extended over most of the Shan states. Some 300 years later, when the British annexed northern Burma, the Shan states were in political disarray. The *saohpas*, or Shan princes, were fighting among themselves, simultaneously attempting to shake off Burmese rule and fighting a losing battle against Kachin raids from the north. British overrule brought some stability and in 1948 Burma gained independence from Britain. The 33 Shan states were formed into a Shan State which had a large degree of autonomy and representation in the national government.

For most Shan the formation of the Shan State represented no radical change, for the largest political unit of traditional Shan society is also the small principality or state. They call it a *mong,* and it is ruled by a *saohpa* and his ministers and officials. The Shan word *mong* means valley state and also traditionally referred to the main town which was the seat of government and the place of the *saohpa.* The traditional political system of Shan society was in many respects similar to European feudalism. The *saohpa* was a lord who owned all the land in his state. All the commoners, the vast majority of the people, owed him allegiance. Local lords, partly territorial chiefs, partly civil servants held office at the pleasure of the *saohpa.* Ambitious and powerful *saohpas* were often, throughout Shan history, able to extend the frontiers of their state at the expense of neighboring *saohpas.* Alternatively a weak ruler of a large state often saw it divided into several smaller ones.

132

Shan myths are full of transformations of men into animals. Here the mythical bird-woman is enacted in a Shan court dance.

Tattoos are both charms to ward off accident and illness, and symbols of manhood. Some girls will not marry a man unless he has been tattooed.

A Shan coffin is obscured by bright paper decorations. On the dead man's tongue lies a coin to pay the spirit ferryman across the river of death.

In a Shan market opium is weighed against silver coins – no paper money is used. A 3lb lump of opium will fetch about $75.

The *saohpa* had the right to demand free labor from his commoners. If, for example, the work was cultivation of the land, then the usual number of days' labor that he demanded was three – one each for transplanting, reaping and threshing the rice. This labor was drawn from all except the very poor within a three-mile limit. The prince's only responsibility in return was to provide his laborers with food throughout those three days. Shan commoners also had to supply their ruling families with enough meat, vegetables and fire-wood for their daily needs. They had to serve as domestic servants, nurse-maids and cooks, gardeners and sweepers. They had to build the *saohpa's* residence and prepare presents for noble weddings, births and deaths. In the past there were villages which were, in effect, service-villages. In exchange for supplying laborers for the prince's fields and servants for his household they were exempted from paying the state taxes. A service-village might have a special duty, perhaps to supply orchids to the prince or grass for his ponies or even the job of tending his elephants. Among the Shan there was no standing army or formal military organization, although able-bodied men might be called at any time to do military service for their prince. In every state certain families or 'circles' supplied the *saohpa's* bodyguard by hereditary right. In return they received houses and land free of taxes.

133

The power of the *saohpa* was not, however, absolute. In the fashion of feudal princedoms it was circumscribed and qualified by his duty to rule according to the conventions and laws of the country. Should even the most powerful prince ignore the advice of his ministers or the Buddhist priests, or violate established customs, then his fate was likely to be deposition or assassination. Elders from the villages and 'circles' had access to the prince's ministers and were thus able to represent to them the wish of the common people. The commoners also had real sanctions which they could impose on an oppressive prince. They could refuse to pay taxes or even migrate to a neighboring state. This sanction was in effect the main check on any prince's rule. The commoners thus ultimately held considerable power.

The Shan are said to be a restless people who frequently move from one state to another. To their mobile, independent character is ascribed their lack of national unity, rivalries between groups and jealousy and distrust between states. There is certainly nothing in the basic conditions of their existence likely to impel them to move. They do not lead harsh lives. Nature is kind to them. There are no great seasonal changes in their country. The valleys in which they make their homes are fertile, water is plentiful and crop yields are high. There is an abundance of vegetable and animal food. Garden fruits and wild fruits have their seasons at different times of the year. Shan settlements are permanent by the nature of their farming, unlike those of the hill tribes. Surpluses allow them to develop trade, and from prosperity springs a degree of cultural sophistication. The river plains and valleys in which Shan villages are built are ideal lands for the paddy wet rice cultivation.

Women rise early in the village to pound the rice. By six o'clock the village is a bustle of activity. The men rise later and seldom leave for the paddy fields before eight or nine o'clock. By then monks are already passing among the villagers, bowls for food-offerings in their hands, as is the custom. Young boys herd the cattle and buffalo while their elder brothers go to the monastery to learn to read and write. Girls stay with their mothers. At various times women and their daughters gather round the village well or stream, washing clothes, gossiping or collecting water. The men and young boys return home before sundown to finish the day's work. If there are no guests men and women eat together, talking of the crops, the rains or the floods and all the other events which touch upon their lives. A favorite topic however is always religion and the mysteries of life and death. *Jatakas,* or tales of the reincarnation of the Buddha, are recounted along with other stories of kings and queens in golden palaces.

The Shan consider themselves more devout Buddhists than their Burmese neighbors, even though it was from them that they first learned the faith. But the Shan, though devout and respectful of Buddhism, could not be said to be strict Buddhists. For alongside this religion, they believe in the existence of spirits and supernatural forces, omens and dreams, lucky and unlucky days. Specialists in the occult will interpret dreams, omens and horoscopes. The Shan believe that everything in nature possesses a soul or spirit which is merely a more refined species of matter, and has power over the growth and development of matter. Stars and planets are not worlds, but divinities whose motions control the destinies of men and all things.

Boys of about 14 are often tattooed in blue designs on their legs, arms, chest or back. These designs may be regarded as charms, and then the skill and occult knowledge of the tattooists are of utmost importance. The tattooing may also be regarded as a sign of manhood, and it is said that girls will ignore potential husbands unless they are tattooed.

The Shan's animistic beliefs are, however, reconciled with their Buddhist beliefs and this leads to many apparent contradictions. Even Shan Buddhist monks are sometimes called in to help combat evil spirits in times of sickness or disaster. Some monasteries have shrines for the local guardian spirits.

The Shan believe that good spirits act as guardians or protective spirits on which they can rely for help in difficult times. A baby is believed to have a spirit-father and spirit-mother who watch over him and protect him from other spirits. The *saohpa* himself has guardian spirits and at one time a riderless pony would accompany the *saohpa* on ceremonial processions. This fully saddled pony, it was believed, carried his protective spirit.

Evil spirits which cause sickness and disaster are usually not permanent resident spirits which have the fortunes of people at heart, but the uneasy shades of dead men who are unable to rest. Evil spirits are liable to interfere with a man at all stages of life, but it seems that there are some times when he is more susceptible. At birth a child must be especially protected. Young people should not be admired too much as this might attract the evil spirits. When he suffers from frequent accidents or illnesses a man will often change his name at appropriate ceremonies to deceive the spirits. And also at the time of traveling to strange places, the Shan are careful. It was once reported that a *saohpa,* on the eve of a journey, made a mock departure in order to evade the spirits.

The Buddhist teachings of the law of Karma appeal to the intellect, but do not deal with the world of spirits and the unknown; nor do they provide any protection against immediate ills and misfortune. One might say that when the Shan are well they appear to be devout Buddhists, but when they are ill they are animists. The element of animism in Shan religion has been compared to a fence built around a lonely house to keep out the tigers at night, to assure the continuance of life and the conditions in which the Buddhism to which they are devoted may be practised.

135

In Shan villages on market day
all other work ceases. Horses
and cattle, silk and home-made
cloth are all sold along with
rice, baskets, meat and fruit.

Negrito
Thailand and Malaya

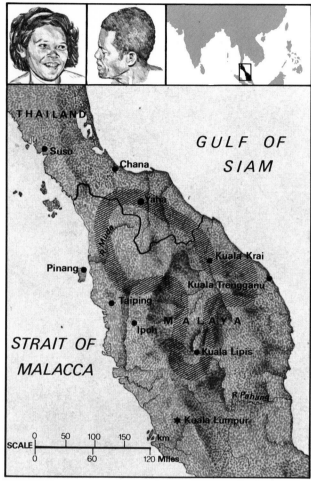

people. Inside they store their few possessions – digging sticks, bamboo pots, wooden mortars, gourds, blow-pipes with poison-tipped arrows, bamboo quivers, combs, rags of clothes made from fibers, various girdles, bracelets and headdresses made of rattan or fiber and usually a piece of steel and quartz and dry fungus kept in a bamboo section for making fish-bait.

Some have taken to a limited temporary kind of cultivation, raising a little hill rice, maize and a few other crops, but they get their main livelihood from hunting small animals: bamboo rats, squirrels, porcupines, flying foxes and especially monkeys.

Women do most of the food gathering. Some of the roots and tubers they gather are poisonous but they neutralize the poison in various ways, and eat them with the vegetables and fruit, bamboo shoots, fungi, larvae, termites and other insects, and honey and molluscs. They roast meat in cleft sticks over the fire, and cook roots or cereals in green bamboo sections. No attempt is made to store food, and animal skins are never used for clothes.

The Negrito's most useful raw material is bamboo. It provides them with cooking utensils, musical instruments, quivers, darts, fishing equipment and countless other articles. Poison for the darts of their blow-pipes is extracted from the resin of the *spoh* tree: injected under the skin of a mammal, it is fatal, causing violent intestinal cramp, but it is harmless to swallow. Negrito smiths heat iron and work with a furnace and bellows.

When a young Negrito is of marriageable age, he chooses a girl, approaches her father, and offers presents or, if he is poor, his labor, to conclude the arrangement. The couple then build themselves a temporary honeymoon shelter in the forest, away from the group.

The ablest man of any group exercises a kind of informal leadership, but only the shaman, the *halak*, holds any distinct office, sometimes inherited from his father, sometimes conferred on him in a dream or by his discovery of a magic stone.

In Negrito dancing, as in the dancers' faces, there is something clearly African. The men make stripes of soot on their faces, chests and backs. Then while the women beat out a rhythm, clapping their hands or beating small drums, the men circle, rush forward, leap at one another, embrace and part, hopping from leg to leg and beating their thighs loudly, shouting and crying out.

Negrito religion is concerned with good and evil spirits that can take the outward forms of birds and animals and which need to be propitiated by various ceremonies and sacrifices. The dead are buried quickly in the jungle. The dead man's spirit is believed to wander around for at least seven days before entering the underworld and the Negrito are mortally afraid of it, and try to prevent it coming to their camp. But once launched upon its journey, it is believed to be on its way to an easier life in a paradisal, fruit-filled region in the west.

Between 2,000 and 3,000 years ago the Negritos almost certainly occupied vast regions of Southeast Asia especially the Malay Peninsula. Today groups survive only in areas of remote and undisturbed forested hill country on the Thai-Malay border, in the Philippines, and in the Andaman islands. Certainly no more than a few thousand survive today but accurate figures are impossible. The shy Negritos are seldom visited. Moreover, they are nomadic, and have retreated into the jungle as lustier peoples of Malay, and latterly Chinese stock, have overtaken their homelands.

In the Thai-Malay border highlands perhaps 2,000 of these timid people continue to live unaffected by outside influences, coming down very occasionally to the nearest Malay or Thai village to exchange their forest produce for tobacco and rice. Each small nomadic group has its own well-defined territory, deep in the forest. When a group moves on it shelters in caves beneath overhanging rocks or in overnight shelters of fern lean-tos. More permanent shelters are made of ferns lashed to saplings. Negrito camps may house from three to a dozen or so of these rough shelters, each of which holds ten to sixty

Only a few thousand Negritos — shy, forest people, seldom contacted — survive out of a population once widespread in South-east Asia.

Small nomadic groups build sapling and fern shelters in forest clearings. They are masters at trapping small game and using the blowpipe.

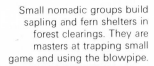

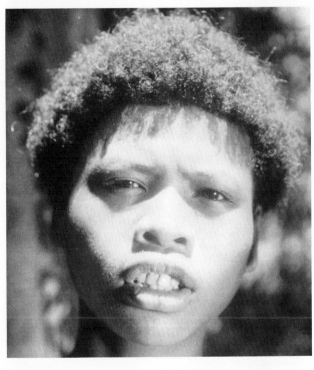

Related to the Negritos, this valley-dwelling Temiar fulfils the shaman's role by dancing himself into a trance to relay spirit voices.

(Center) The markedly African aspect of Negritos suggests a once global distribution of negroid types in the then inhabited tropical world.

On the walls of a jungle cave near Lenggong in Perak, northern Malaya, Negrito drawings recall prehistoric cave drawings in Europe.

13

Glossary
to the peoples of South-east Asia

The strongest forces in the early ethnic and cultural evolution of the peoples of mainland South-east Asia came from the neighboring sub-continents of China and India. The countries of South-east Asia have for centuries absorbed overspills of population from China and have attracted the attentions of Chinese empire builders. The influence of India on the development of South-east Asia has largely been less direct. The Indians came by sea, not land, and neither predominantly as migrants nor as conquerors. Their influence has been more cultural than ethnic.

From as early as 2,000 years ago the primitive hunting and gathering culture of South-east Asian aboriginal peoples like the Negritos was, in favorable areas, progressively displaced by sedentary cultivation of wet rice. The new wet-rice agriculture, stimulated by contact with Chinese and Indians, provided the material basis for a higher level of civilization.

Most South-east Asians today are descendants of migrants. More recent migrations were of tribal minority peoples in South China driven south, by Han Chinese expansion, from the far north-west. Tribes displaced to the south pushed the earlier inhabitants into the less fertile uplands which were often suitable only for slash-and-burn agriculture. They were invariably less culturally advanced than their Chinese contemporaries in the rear, but tended to be more advanced than the people they were driven among. The Tai, for example, had already acquired a cultural sophistication from their Chinese neighbors before they moved south and came to dominate much of Thailand during the 13th and 14th centuries. This pattern of Chinese influence has continued even into the 20th century. The Meo, who now live in Thailand and neighboring areas, migrated south from China.

The Indians on the other hand came to South-east Asia by way of the seas. By the dawn of the Christian era they had discovered sea routes even to the coast of China. During the first millennium AD Hindu and Buddhist beliefs, along with the art of writing, many technological innovations and the rudiments of urbanization spread from the delta lands of South-east Asia inland via the great rivers. The process of Indianization gradually spread until the greater part of the lowlands had come under the influence of Indian religious beliefs.

ACHANG *Population:* 1,000. Language group: Tibeto-Burman. The Achang live in northern Burma along the Chinese frontier, and over the border in Yunnan. They are shifting cultivators of wet rice. In winter many travel to the Burmese Shan (pages 130–135) states to work as carpenters, blacksmiths, or in the Mogok ruby mines. They make fine plows and swords from local iron. In their Buddhist practices, customs and dress they are like the Shan. They have intermarried extensively with their Chinese neighbors.

ALAK *Population:* 2,000. Language group: Mon-Khmer. The Alak inhabit parts of the Attopeu and Saravane provinces in Laos. They cultivate dry, upland rice, areca trees, betel vines and tobacco and are skilful weavers of red-and-blue cloth. Some men work as wage-laborers. They live in circular villages centered on a communal house, with sacrificial posts outside. They make buffalo sacrifices and village sorcerers predict the future through necromancy.

ANNAMESE (see VIETNAMESE)

BAHNAR (pages 24-39)

BIH *Population:* 8,000. Language group: Cham. The Bih live south of the Darlac plateau near the lower Krong Kno river in South Vietnam. They grow rice in paddy fields. In some villages, near fine clay beds, women make pots for domestic use.

BRAO *Population:* 40,000. Language group: Mon-Khmer. The Brao are distributed over a large upland area of central Cambodia. A few emigrated across the Mekong river into Thailand. They are slash-and-burn cultivators of dry rice, and fish to supplement their diet. Their villages – traditionally round, fortified and centered around a communal house – have, since French colonial administration, tended to split into smaller hamlets.

BURMESE (pages 98-111)

CHAM *Population:* 125,000. Language group: Cham. Most Cham live along the south-central coastal plain of Vietnam and in Cambodia around Tonle Sap. They are the descendants of the ancient Vietnamese kingdom of Champa; the ancestors of the Cambodian Cham were refugees from this ancient kingdom. They have now adopted many aspects of Khmer (pages 70-77) culture while those in Vietnam have adopted many Vietnamese customs. Cham agriculture is dominated by market gardening. In Vietnam they breed buffalo, goats and chickens but because of their Brahman origins do not raise cattle. The Cambodian Cham are fishermen and cultivators who grow cotton, indigo and sesame. Many make jewelry and sculpture; some are boatbuilders. Their women weave in silk and make hats. Some Cham are Muslims; some have a religion derived from Brahmanism and Islam; others retain a traditional ancestor cult.

CHAOBON *Population:* 3,000. Language group: Mon-Khmer. The Chaobon live in villages in Khorat, Chaiyaphum, and Phetchabun provinces east of the Sak river valley in central Thailand. Most cultivate wet rice although a few villages still grow dry rice and maize on hill clearings. Their ancient animistic beliefs and practices have largely given way to Buddhism adopted from the Thais.

CHIN *Population:* 400,000. Language group: Tibeto-Burman. The Chin include many groups in western Burma and parts of the Irrawaddy valley. Their main crops are rice and maize. They also cultivate legumes, cucurbits (gourd plants), sugar cane, spices, and root crops. In small plots they grow bananas, garlic, chilies and indigo. In the hill villages the Chin are avid fishermen: some claim to know 16 types of fish poison. In these hill villages locally-grown cotton is ginned, spun, woven on a belt loom, and dyed. Many Chin also make pottery, iron and baskets. For centuries they have depended on buying iron, salt and other prestige goods. Their settlements range from large villages to scattered, isolated houses among the hills. The Chin have been in contact with and under the influence of Burmese and Indians for many years. Some are Hindus, some Christian and some preserve their ancient beliefs.

CHONG *Population:* 5,000. Language group: Mon-Khmer. The Chong live in the border area of Thailand and Cambodia, south-west of Tonle Sap, and in parts of the Cardamom mountains. They are primarily rice farmers, but some breed cattle. They also grow cardamom which is transported on pack-bullocks down from the hills to trade in the market town. The Chong were once a widespread people, but have now been largely assimilated into Khmer (pages 70-77) society.

CHRAU *Population:* 15,000. Language group: Mon-Khmer. The Chrau villages are north-east of Saigon in the southern Annam mountains in South Vietnam. Mostly slash-and-burn rice farmers, their traditional way of life has been much disrupted by the effects of war in Vietnam.

CHURU *Population:* 10,000. Language group: Cham. The Churu live near the Dran valley between Da Lat and Phan Rang in South Vietnam. They have had extensive contact with the Cham (q.v.), from whom they learnt paddy cultivation of rice. They use buffalos and plows in the broad valleys but they rent the slopes to the Kil (q.v.).

CUA (see KHUA)

HALANG *Population:* 10,000. Language group: Mon-Khmer. Halang villages are built along the Se Son river in the Attopeu Province of southern Laos, and in the Kontum Province of Vietnam. They are farmers who cultivate upland rice, maize and tobacco. They are also craftsmen who make baskets and in one

village, Dak Kon, fine wooden platters which are sold to the Lao (pages 40-45). The villages often have one or more communal houses. The building of a communal house was once initiated by a human sacrifice. The victim was crushed beneath the main pillar as it was set in the ground. Although the Halong no longer inaugurate a new communal house in this way, their religious beliefs are still animistic.

HALANG DOAN *Population:* 1,000. Language group: Mon-Khmer. The Halang Doan live in Attopeu province, on the Kasseng plateau and left banks of the Se Kamane and Dak Robay rivers in Laos. They are slash-and-burn farmers who grow dry upland rice. They work in metal and trade with neighboring groups. Their villages are fortified, the long houses built on piles and grouped in an oval about a communal house.

HAW *Population:* 1,000. Language group: Sinitic. The Chinese hill farmers and traders who originate from Yunnan province and now live in northern Thailand and Laos are called 'Haw' by the local Tai. Their advanced agricultural techniques and methods of animal husbandry are admired by other hill peoples of the region.

HPON *Population:* 1,000. Language group: Tibeto-Burman. The Hpon live along the Irrawaddy river between Bhamo and Sinbo in north Burma. They are a small group of mixed cultural and linguistic background. They are shifting cultivators of rice. They also fish and work occasionally cutting timber. Others work as 'trackers', assisting the passage of ships through the narrow gorge of the Irrawaddy. They are now Buddhists.

HRE *Population:* 27,000. Language group: Mon-Khmer. The Hre live in the mountainous region of central Vietnam, inland from the coastal city of Quang Ngai. They are primarily slash-and-burn rice farmers. The ownership of every rice terrace passes from father to son, and in every village the rights of ownership are strictly preserved.

HROY *Population:* 10,000. Language group: Cham. The Hroy live east of Cheo Reo in

South Vietnam. They are slash-and-burn cultivators of rice, who also grow maize, millet, pumpkins and fruits. Their houses are built on piles. The Hroy have extensively intermarried with the larger Bahnar (pages 24-39) and Jarai (pages 24-39) groups, and lost much of their separate identity.

JARAI (pages 24-39)

JEH (pages 24-39)

KACHIN *Population:* 400,000. Language group: Tibeto-Burman. The Kachin, who include the Atsi, Lashi, and Maru, live in the rough mountainous country of the east and central Kachin state and in parts of Shan state in northern Burma. They are mainly slash-and-burn farmers who grow rice, maize, millet, pumpkins, cotton and opium poppies. They fish with traps and poison, and hunt during the cold season. They breed animals only for sacrifice. Most Kachin villages have a sacred grove marked by prayer posts and shrines to the spirits. They have no markets, but trade at nearby Shan, Burmese and Chinese towns. There are two types of community – the *gumsa* which are aristocratic and stratified, and the *gumlao,* democratic and egalitarian. But a man is not bound to the

139

community into which he is born. Most Kachin still observe ancient and traditional beliefs and rituals.

KADU *Population:* 40,000. Language group: Tibeto-Burman. The Kadu live in north Burma, mainly in the Katha district near the Assam frontier. They grow rice on irrigated terraces, together with some tea and cotton. They build their villages on the spurs of hills overlooking the valley floors. Many Kadu men work for Burmese lumber firms as elephant drivers or wood-cutters. Through intermarriage with their Burmese neighbors they have assimilated much of the broader Burmese culture. They have also, at least superficially, adopted the Buddhist religion.

KALO *Population:* 20,000. Language group: Mon-Khmer. The Kalo inhabit the central Vietnamese highlands inland from the coastal city of Quang Tri. Predominantly slash-and-burn rice farmers, they have had considerable contact with the coastal Vietnamese as well as with neighboring groups.

KAREN (pages 126-129)

KASSENG *Population:* 4,000. Language group: Mon-Khmer. The Kasseng live in the higher parts of a plateau between Nam Touei and Nam Ang in Saravane province,

Laos. They are slash-and-burn agriculturalists who grow upland rice, maize and tobacco. Their villages are arranged around a communal house and encompassed by an oval wall. Many Kasseng weave cloth and produce black lacquered shields covered with tin to trade.

KATANG *Population:* 13,000. Language group: Mon-Khmer. The Katang, one of the Kha group, live in parts of southern Laos near the South Vietnam border. They grow rice both by slash-and-burn agriculture and in irrigated paddy fields. Maize is an important secondary crop and they keep buffalo as draft animals for paddy cultivation. A Katang village usually consists of a communal house and between two and five long houses built in pilings and arranged in a square or triangle. They hunt deer, gaur (wild ox), and trap wild pigs. Only small animals like monkeys and squirrels are shot with the crossbow.

KATU *Population:* 25,000. Language group: Mon-Khmer. The Katu live mostly on the valley slopes of the Song Giang, Cai and Boung in the hilly interior of central Vietnam from Da Nang to the border with southern Laos. They grow dry rice, manioc and maize, and collect wild fruit, roots, and edible leaves from the forest. In the middle of their circular, stockaded villages stand carved sacrificial posts to which animals are tied during ritual sacrifice. Human blood sacrifices still survive in some places as well. The central communal house functions as a village religious center for the worship of many spirits. It is believed to be the sacred dwelling place of the souls of their ancestors.

KHMER (pages 70-77)

KHMU *Population:* 105,000. Language group: Mon-Khmer. The Khmu are the largest group in northern Laos, and the only one in Luang Prabang and Xieng Khouang provinces. In Thailand they live mostly in the northern Nan province near the Laos border. Most Khmu are agriculturalists, whose staple food of rice is supplemented by hunting, gathering, trapping and fishing. They are skilled weavers of baskets, trays, net bags, and stools made of thin strips of

bamboo and rattan. They trade through Lao (q.v.) merchants. Although some are Buddhist or Christian most adhere to their own tribal beliefs.

KHUA *Population:* 1,000. Language group: Mon-Khmer. The Khua or Cua live in small mountainside villages in the Quang Binh province of North Vietnam. They are slash-and-burn farmers, who will soon be indistinguishable as a separate group.

KHUN *Population:* 35,000. Language group: Tai. The Khun are a Shan (pages 130-135) people living in and around the old walled town of Keng Tung in the northern Burmese state of Keng Tung. Only a few live in north Thailand. They are predominantly wet-rice farmers and cattle breeders who also cultivate opium poppies which have to be smuggled into Thailand. The Khun are Theravada Buddhists whose temples and rituals reveal both Burmese and Chinese influences.

KIL *Population:* 11,000. Language group: Mon-Khmer. The Kil, a subgroup of the Muong (q.v.), live north-east of Da Lat in South Vietnam. They are slash-and-burn agriculturalists who often have to lease land from the neighboring Churu. Hunting and gathering are both necessary for their survival – but they are also known for their fine basketwork.

KUI *Population:* 110,000. Language group: Mon-Khmer. Most of the Kui live in the Thai provinces of Surin, Sisaket, Ubon and Roi Et. In Cambodia they live in the northern Siem Reap-Kampong-Thom area near the Thai border. They represent an ancient population who came into the region before the Tai (pages 82-91) and Khmer (pages 70-77). Although some continue to use primitive methods of hoe agriculture, most have adopted the permanent wet-rice cultivation of their lowland neighbors. In some areas they have acquired a reputation as elephant hunters and iron forgers. Most of the Kui have adopted the Buddhism of their neighbors, but there are still some who preserve their tribal beliefs. In Cambodia their extensive intermarriage with their neighbors threatens their separate identity.

LAMET *Population:* 6,000. Language group: Mon-Khmer. The hill-dwelling Lamet live along the Haut Mekong-Luang Prabang boundary in north-west Laos. They are almost totally dependent on rice farming but supplement their diet by gathering wild roots, shoots and buds. They raise red pepper, millet, taro, and vegetables by slash-and-burn cultivation which makes no use of animals or the plow. They keep bees for honey and beeswax, an important item of trade. They trade in rice, wine, brandy, fermented tea balls, powdered deer horn and dried bears' bladders (the last two are used in Chinese pharmacy). In their villages there is a class of wealthy men, known as the *lem*. Wealth is reckoned in buffalo, gongs and bronze drums. They have largely retained their tribal beliefs.

LAO (pages 40-45)

LAT *Population:* 2,000. Language group: Mon-Khmer. The Lat live near Da Lat in South Vietnam. They are a small group of slash-and-burn farmers, with little to distinguish them from their neighbors.

LAYA *Population:* 2,000. Language group: Mon-Khmer. The Laya (or La-Gia) live inland from Phan Thiet in South Vietnam. They are a relatively small group of slash-and-burn farmers.

LII *Population:* 60,000. Language group: Tai. The Lii live in the Keng Tung State of Burma, and in northern Laos and Vietnam, and about 18 million live in China. They are primarily wet-rice farmers. Domestic animals contribute an important part of their diet, along with rice, beans and vegetables. Fish are eaten whenever available. The Lii everywhere are addicted to opium.

LOLO *Population:* 18,000. Language group: Tibeto-Burman. The Lolo live in the North Vietnamese upland areas of Lai Chau, Lao Cay, and Yen Bay. There are a few in north Thailand, Laos and Burma, and over three million in China. Most of the Lolo in Indochina are slash-and-burn rice farmers who cultivate the slopes although some grow rice in paddy fields and the lower lands of river valleys. They also grow maize, tobacco, and opium poppies, and keep bees for honey which they sell. They weave, dye, and distil alcohol. They have adopted some of the religious beliefs of the neighboring groups of Meo (pages 92-97), Yao (pages 46-49), and Thai (q.v.). They use little baskets, or *lolo,* to house the souls of their ancestors.

LOVEN *Population:* 20,000. Language group: Mon-Khmer. The Loven live on the Bolovens plateau between Paksane and Thateng in southern Laos. They are slash-and-burn cultivators of upland rice, maize, red peppers, yams and Irish potatoes (introduced by the French). They have had extensive contact with Lao (pages 40-45), with Europeans who established plantations in their territory, and with Chinese merchants to whom they sell their coffee crops. Many Loven are skilled woodworkers. And although many Loven have turned to Buddhism, many others still retain their traditional beliefs.

LUA *Population:* 10,000. Language group: Mon-Khmer. The Lua live in the flat plateau district of Meahongsorn and Chiengmai provinces in northern Thailand. Where they can cultivate wet rice, the Lua build large, permanent villages. They breed buffalo, but only for plowing since they are mainly vegetarian. In the more remote forest clearings they grow dry rice and chilies. They observe their traditional religion alongside Buddhism.
(see pages 122-125)

MA *Population:* 28,000. Language group: Mon-Khmer. The Ma live on both banks of the elbow of the Upper Donnai River in South Vietnam. This fertile valley is the heart of their country which they farm by slash-and-burn. Some hunt the game which abounds on the right bank where there is less vegetation.

MAN (see YAO)

MENAM *Population:* 5,000. Language group: Mon-Khmer. The Menam inhabit the valley of the Upper Song Tranh River in the Laos border area of Quang Ngai province in South Vietnam. Predominantly wet and dry rice farmers, they live in closeknit, fortified villages. They collect medicinal herbs and cinnamon which they then trade, primarily with the Duane and Noar groups. They retain their traditional tribal beliefs.

MEO (pages 92-97)

MIAO (see MEO)

MNONG (pages 24-39)

MOKEN (pages 112-119)

MON *Population:* 400,000. Language group: Mon-Khmer. The Mon live chiefly in the northern Tenasserim panhandle in Burma, also in Thailand around Bangkok and in the lower valley of the Mae Khlong. They are primarily peasant rice farmers, although fish and fish products are an essential part of their diet. They rear domestic animals including cattle, buffalo, pigs and horses. Most are Theravada Buddhists, although some hold Hindu, and others preserve indigenous pagan beliefs.

MUONG *Population:* 300,000. Language group: Mon-Khmer. The Muong live over a wide area of uplands on the south-western fringe of the Red River delta in North Vietnam. Primarily peasant rice farmers, they also cultivate maize, sesame, manioc, tomatoes and grapefruit. Many Muong families also cultivate cotton. Fishing, with a variety of fish traps, is an important means of supplementing the diet. The Muong believe in many supernatural beings, which they contact through diviners, healers and male and female magicians.

NEGRITOS (pages 136-137)

NEUA *Population:* 40,000. Language group: Tai. The Neua live in north-east Laos. They are subsistence farmers, growing both wet and dry rice. They trade extensively with surrounding peoples, and are Buddhists.

NGEH *Population:* 3,000. Language group: Mon-Khmer. Most Ngeh live in the Saravane province of Laos. They are peasant farmers, cultivating wet rice in irrigated fields, and they slash-and-burn higher lands to grow dry rice. They also weave fine cloths, and build long houses on piles.

NGOK PA (see SEMANG)

NGUNG BO *Population:* 3,000. Language group: Mon-Khmer. There are about twenty Ngung Bo villages along the banks of the Rao Lao and upper Se Kong rivers in southern Laos. They are peasant farmers who cultivate tobacco as well as wet and dry rice. They produce baskets and sometimes sell buffalo to the Vietnamese.

NHANG *Population:* 12,000. Language group: Tai. The Nhang live in North Vietnam along the Chinese border, concentrated beside the Claire, Song Chay and Red rivers. Predominantly peasant farmers, they cultivate terraces with crops including rice, maize, indigo, sugar and

cotton. They live in settlements of ten to twelve farmsteads: although they have their own village headmen, they often live under the political dominance of a neighboring group. They largely retain their indigenous beliefs.

NOANG *Population:* 9,000. Language group: Cham. The Noang live south-east of Da Lat in South Vietnam. They are slash-and-burn rice farmers. They have male and female sorcerers who they call *bojou* and have largely retained their tribal beliefs, although their traditional way of life has been seriously disrupted by war in Vietnam.

NOP *Population:* 2,000. Language group: Mon-Khmer. The Nop live south-west of Djiring town in South Vietnam. They are slash-and-burn rice agriculturalists who have long had close ties with the local Vietnamese.

OY *Population:* 5,000. Language group: Mon-Khmer. The Oy inhabit the slopes of the Bolovens plateau in Attopeu province, Laos. They are peasant rice farmers, and breed domestic animals. Some Oy build pentagonal houses with roofs often elaborately decorated with wooden carvings of buffalo horns. The Oy often construct bamboo aqueducts. They have a well-defined taboo or *kalam* system. Most of the Oy are Buddhists; some villages are Roman Catholic.

PADUANG (pages 120-121)

PALAUNG *Population:* 150,000. Language group: Mon-Khmer. The Palaung live in Burma chiefly in the southern Kachin state and in north-western Shan state. Most are subsistence slash-and-burn rice farmers, and plant their fields with beans, peas, sesame, maize and hemp. They grow wet rice wherever possible, cultivate, prepare and trade tea, and trade horses. They have a state system with a prince at its head. Annually the prince, elders and people assemble at a great festival. Nominally Buddhist, they also believe in many traditional spirits.

PANTHAY *Population:* 3,000. Language group: Sinitic. The Panthay are nomadic Muslim Chinese muleteers of the Burma-China frontier area, with scattered settlements throughout the Wa States-Kengtung area of Burma. They often take their goods caravans as far as Rangoon and Moulmein. Chiefly traders, who have had extensive contacts with other groups, they cultivate enough rice for subsistence.

PAK-TAI *Population:* 1,500,000. Language group: Tai. Pak-Tai live in the extreme south of Thailand and are said to intermarry with both Malays and Negritos (pages 136-137). They are predominantly rice paddy farmers and cattle breeders, but also work as rubber planters and fishermen.

PA-Y *Population:* 600. Language group: Tai. Most Pa-Y live in the mountainous region of Pa Kha and around Muong Khuong near the Chinese-North Vietnam border. They are predominantly subsistence rice farmers and have extensively intermarried with the Nung. They practise an ancestor cult and believe in many supernatural spirits.

PEAR *Population:* 10,000. Language group: Mon-Khmer. The Pear live on the northern slopes of the Cardamom mountains and are widely intermingled with the Cambodian population. Predominantly slash-and-burn rice farmers, they also gather wild yams, bamboo leaves and shoots, and fish and hunt. They live in scattered clusters of farmsteads. The Pear are rapidly disappearing as an identifiable ethnic group.

P'U NOI *Population:* 20,000. Language group: Mon-Khmer. The P'u Noi inhabit highlands in northern Laos. They are slash-and-burn farmers who grow rice, maize, tobacco and cotton, and raise buffalo, goats and pigs. They eat earth almost every day as a remedy for diarrhea.

RAGLAI *Population:* 40,000. Language group: Cham. The northern Raglai occupy the highlands inland from Nhatran in South Vietnam. The southern Raglai live inland from Phan Rang south of Dalat. Both groups are slash-and-burn rice farmers sometimes known as Orang Glai or 'men of the forest'. The Raglai village of Choah is a religious sanctuary to which sorcerers make annual pilgrimages.

RENAGO *Population:* 6,000. Language group: Mon-Khmer. The Renago live in the South Vietnamese highlands near Kontum. They are slash-and-burn cultivators of rice, but are also fishers, hunters and gatherers. Similar to, and perhaps part of, the Bahnar group (q.v.) they retain indigenous beliefs.

RHADE (pages 24-39)

SAOCH *Population:* 300. Language group: Mon-Khmer. The Saoch live along Kompong Smach river in Cambodia. They grow enough paddy rice to sell a surplus to surrounding Khmer (pages 70-77) for whom the Saoch also work as laborers. They fish, hunt and trap. Long considered unfriendly and aloof, they have increasingly come into contact with the Khmer, borrowing much from their culture and occasionally marrying Khmer women. Their cult centers on a stone fetish in the woods.

SAPUAN *Population:* 1,000. Language group: Mon-Khmer. The Sapuan live along the border of Laos. Predominantly wet-rice

cultivators, they also fish and rear livestock. Their villages are scattered farmsteads built on piles. The Lao (pages 40-45) have mixed with and influenced them very much, as has Buddhism.

SEDANG *Population:* 80,000. Language group: Mon-Khmer. The Sedang inhabit the South Vietnamese highlands to the north-west of Kontum. They are subsistence rice farmers, who also fish, hunt and rear water-buffalo and pigs. The Sedang blacksmith is believed to have magical powers. The soul of a buffalo killed with an iron spear goes to the gods, whereas normally it would join the soul of the man performing the sacrifice. Until recently, the Sedang were cannibals. The most powerful supernatural beings in the Sedang religion are Grandfather and Grandmother Knda, the creators.

SEMANG (pages 136-137)

SHAN (pages 130-135)

SO *Population:* 10,000. Language group: Mon-Khmer. The So live along the Mekong in Thailand and Laos. They are predominantly

subsistence rice farmers. They fish and hunt tigers, gaur (wild ox), panthers, deer and wild boar, mainly with the crossbow. The So weave much of their cloth, make their own baskets and crossbows and some are skilled blacksmiths. The So are Theravada Buddhists, attending the pagodas of the neighboring Laotian Tai.

SOU *Population:* 1,000. Language group: Mon-Khmer. The small group of Sou live on the plain at the confluence of the Sekong and Se Kamane rivers in Laos. They are peasant rice farmers who also fish and do a little metalwork. Their small villages are strung out along the river banks. They believe in many traditional spirits.

SOUEI *Population:* 9,000. Language group: Mon-Khmer. The Souei live in Muong Lao Ngam and near Thateng in southern Laos. They are primarily peasant rice farmers, who trade with the Lao (pages 40-45). Their religion is a combination of Buddhism and spirit cults, although some villages have been converted to Roman Catholicism.

SRE *Population:* 30,000. Language group: Mon-Khmer. The Sre villages are near Djiring at the southern end of the Annam Cordillera in South Vietnam. With buffalos and plows they cultivate wet-rice in the bottom land of their upland valleys. They live in thatch-roofed houses built on low piles. Predominantly a pagan tribe, every Sre village has both male and female sorcerers.

STIENG (pages 24-39)

TAI *Population:* 19,900,000. Language group: Tai. In Thailand there are 18 million Tai and there are quite large groups of Tai speakers in Laos, where they are known as the Lao (pages 40-45), and in Vietnam. The Vietnamese Tai are known as Black Tai, White Tai and Red Tai, identifiable by the color of the clothes the women wear. There is another small group of Tai in northern Laos and Thailand who retain their tribal customs and way of life. They are known as the Phutai. The Phutai and the Vietnamese Tai

adhere to their traditional religious beliefs but those in Laos and Thailand practise Theravada Buddhism mixed with traces of Hindu beliefs.
(pages 82-91)

TAU-OI *Population:* 11,000. Language group: Mon-Khmer. The Tau-Oi live in Saravane province, Laos and in the mountainous area inland from the Vietnamese city of Quang Tri. Predominantly slash-and-burn rice farmers, they also fish and a few work as wage-laborers. They live in circular, fortified villages with a communal house at the center. The Tau-Oi believe in many different spirits, although a number of their villages have been converted to Roman Catholicism.

THO *Population:* 430,000. Language group: Tai. The Tho live to the north and north-east of the Red River delta in North Vietnam as far as the Chinese border. Predominantly shifting cultivators, they also grow cash crops of tobacco, cotton, indigo and opium. They are celebrated breeders of horses, which they trade, together with aniseed and turpentine. An élite, known as the Tho-ti, are descendants of Vietnamese mandarins sent into the area in the 17th century. Only these have an organized Buddhist religion. Other Tho have ill-defined beliefs in Buddhist deities, mixed with some Confucianism and Taoism.

T'IN *Population:* 35,000. Language group: Mon-Khmer. The T'in live in the northern mountains of Nan province, north Thailand, and across the border in Sayaboury province, Laos. The T'in are a people who are often on the move and live close to starvation. Slash-and-burn farmers, they are forced by uncertain crop yields to rely heavily on gathering and selling forest products or their own labor. They also sell pickled tea leaves and rattan mats for cash. Some T'in villages exploit salt wells at the headwaters of the Nan river. Only a few T'in near the lowlands have adopted Buddhism.

T'OU LAO *Population:* 600. Language group: Tai. The T'ou Lao inhabit the Upper Song Chay river area of North Vietnam near the Chinese border. They are a Tai (q.v.) tribal group of peasant rice farmers, akin to the surrounding Meo (pages 92-97). Some are also fishermen and boatmen.

TRUNG-CHA *Population:* 200. Language group: Tai. This small group live near the Chinese border in North Vietnam. Predominantly peasant rice farmers, they also specialize in forging, carpentry, stone-cutting, jewelry, ceramics and weaving. Some of their villages are mixed settlements with Nhang (q.v.) and Tho (q.v.) families as well.

VIETNAMESE (see pages 14-23, 50-69)

WA *Population:* 335,000. Language group: Mon-Khmer. The Wa live in the southern

Shan states of Burma, particularly along the upper Salween river. The lowland Wa are peasant farmers living in large, heavily fortified villages. Their chief crop is the opium poppy, grown largely for trade. Their hill rice is used entirely for alcohol. Most 'tame' Wa are Buddhist; the 'wild' Wa, isolated in the mountains, have been headhunters at least as recently as 1935.

YAO (pages 46-49)

YUAN (see LAO)

YUMBRI *Population:* 200. Language group: Mon-Khmer. The Yumbri are a group of small bands of nomadic gatherers in northern Thailand. Moving in very small family groups, they frequent remote mountain tracts covered by dense tropical jungle. They are known as the 'spirits of the yellow leaves', which alludes to their belief that when the leaf roof of their flimsy shelters turns yellow they must leave the camp site. They eat wild fruits, leaves, roots, wild yams, snails, caterpillars, rats and lizards. Since they avoid streams, which they believe are inhabited by evil spirits, they can eat no fish. The Yumbri are close to extinction. A number of the hill tribes shoot them on sight, and tigers, disease and malnutrition take their annual toll.

All population figures are approximate.